# Germany Tomorrow

# CONTENTS

# CONTENTS

PART THREE

# THE NEW ORDER      117

STRUCTURE OF GERMAN SOCIALISM

# CONTENTS

# CONTENTS

# BIOGRAPHICAL AND
# BIBLIOGRAPHICAL NOTE

OTTO STRASSER, a Bavarian, was born on September 10, 1897. His brother, Gregor, five years older, was killed by Goering's orders (Hitler accepted responsibility) in the Blood Bath of June 30, 1934. Both brothers were Nazis at a time when the National Socialists were really socialists as well as nationalists, and they remained socialists after Hitler had dropped this part of his creed. That was the untoward fact that led to Gregor's murder. Five years before this Otto had broken with Hitler; on May 10, 1933, he left Germany to become a refugee in Austria, subsequently in Czechoslovakia, Switzerland, and France (where he now resides).

Otto Strasser's ideas on German Socialism were incorporated in a book *Aufbau des deutschen Sozialismus* published in 1931, second edition 1936. The bulk of it appears in Part Three of the present volume, being essential to the author's presentation of Germany Tomorrow. Part One, 'Is Revolution in Germany Possible?', and Part Two 'Liquidation of the War (Peace Proposals of Tomorrow's Germany)', were written at the turn of the year, i.e. well after the outbreak of the war, expressly for the present book. All three parts, and the Appendix matter, speak for themselves, so nothing more need be said about bibliography.

Otto Strasser played an active part in the previous war, joining the Bavarian army as a volunteer on August 2, 1914, rising from the ranks to become a lieutenant, decorated, and twice wounded. He took the degree of Doctor of Law in 1921, and for a time held an official post under the Weimar Republic. Then he was appointed legal adviser to an industrial concern in Berlin. For some years after this he was editor-in-chief (during the gradual rise of the Nazis) of most of the North German periodicals of the National Socialist Party. After his breach with Hitler he founded the Black Front, an anti-Hitler organization, which aims also (and chiefly) at promoting 'German Socialism'. It plays a considerable part in this book, and will perhaps play a still more considerable part in Germany Tomorrow, and in Europe the Day after Tomorrow. Since in Germany Today assassination has a recognized function in politics, it is not surprising that even as a refugee Otto Strasser has had several 'narrow squeaks'. But he still continues his reasoned (and bloodless) campaign for promoting the downfall of the Hitler System and the upbuilding of German Socialism — a campaign with which *Germany Tomorrow* has much to do. The book is addressed, not only to Germans, but to all 'Good Europeans'.

EDEN AND CEDAR PAUL

London
*May Day, 1940*

# PREFACE

THIS war is the inevitable outcome of the Hitler System. For the last ten years, and especially since Hitler seized power, I have been indefatigably trying to demonstrate as much in countless publications.

Regard for historical truth makes it essential to state that Hitler's seizure of power was part of that Germano-European development to which I have given the general name of the 'German Revolution', by which I mean the birth of a new order in politics, economics, and civilization. Issuing from Germany, this will to a greater or less extent transform the established European system even as, at their respective times, did the English Revolution and the French.

From this outlook we can understand the otherwise inexplicable mistakes and shortcomings of the statesmen of other lands, beginning with Dollfuss and Schuschnigg, going on to Hodscha and Beck, next to François Poncet and Nevile Henderson, and last of all to the men of the 'Peace of Munich' — since had it not been for these mistakes and shortcomings Adolf Hitler would never have been able to carry out his work of destruction — and even so we have to recognize that such work of destruction has been and is the necessary prelude to the up-building of the new order which is the meaning of this, as of every revolution. Contemplation based upon a study of the philosophy of history does much to lessen the blame attaching to the German people for the Hitler System and the war to which it has given rise. The

GERMANY TOMOR]

# PREFACE

Germans may have to shoulder the greater share of blame, but their share is only a part of the general load which must be assigned in varying degrees to the policies of other countries than Germany.

More important, however, than the assignment of multifarious shares of blame to Hitler and his war (an assignment justified and restricted by our historical outlook), is the no less inevitable certainty we derive that Hitler and his war will be defeated.

And how?

Certainly if we regard, as I and my friends do, the Hitler System (and for our purposes that includes the civil war in Europe which the Hitler System has brought about) as a necessary stage in the transition from a decaying old order to an evolving new one, as the epoch during which effete forms are being swept away — why then we shall have the joyful conviction that such an epoch of destruction cannot possibly be lasting. It will come to an end as soon as the old and the worm-eaten have really been swept away, and as soon as the new and the young that are everywhere germinating beneath the surface of things come clearly to light.

From this outlook Hitler is really no more than the testing 'hammer of God' with which men and things are tapped to discover whether life persists in them, whether they still have faith, will, strength, and the power of renewal. Where these good qualities are lacking, the hammer breaks the old forms to powder — even as, in scripture, the tree which bore no fruit was to be ruthlessly cut down. But when fruit-bearing is still possible, the will to and the power for renewal will

16

infallibly spring up after the hard testing of these blows; under new forms, but in the old spirit, the spirit of the 'Mothers' in *Faust* which dwells in the depths of our soul, the soul of every human being, the soul of every nation, the soul of the West. Revolutionary in form, conservative in substance, is the policy that derives from such a method of contemplation.

Victory over Hitler and his system of destruction, victory in this war over the powers of destruction, is no less certain than were the coming of Hitler and this war; and both spring from the necessity and the nature of the 'German Revolution'.

Three questions necessarily arise for consideration after such an outlook has been defined, three questions which must be answered before we can be sure that we have more to guide us than mere faith in the future; three questions which the non-German world above all will put, in order to learn what lies behind this contention, and what the foreign world has to expect from our 'German Revolution':

(1) Is a revolution at all possible in Germany?

(2) What would the ideas of such a 'German Revolution' be as regards the liquidation of the war?

(3) What sort of aspect would the new order have in Germany?

The importance of these questions, and the warrant we have for putting them, are all the more palpable because war prevails, so that men are summoned to battle, wish to know and are entitled to know what they are fighting for and why they are making sacrifices.

The aim of this book is to answer these three questions,

to answer them as accurately as possible and with a full sense of responsibility imposed on us by the deadly earnestness of our time.

It arises from the circumstances of the case that the answers to questions (1) and (2) must 'date', must arise out of the extant military situation; while nevertheless they also arise out of the spirit of the new order, which forces itself into the light independently of Hitler's regime and Hitler's war.

Nothing can prove this more convincingly than the fact that the plans for the new order in Germany were drafted years before the Hitler System, and therefore longer still before the war. They were drafted in their main lines, and constituted the written program of a large and active political movement in the Reich.

As Douglas Reed shows in his instructive book *Nemesis?*, these main lines formed the substantial content of the so-called Hanover Program which was adopted in 1925 as the program of the North German group of the National Socialists, and became the cause of my breach with Hitler. After 1930 it was the official program of the Black Front, and was published as such in 1931 in the first edition of my own book *Aufbau des deutschen Sozialismus*.

The most important chapters of that book comprise Part Three of the present work, and show the latter to be in no sense a degenerate form of concession to the present war and its expected result.

To emphasize this I have deliberately left standing certain sections that have grown obsolete during the last ten years, sections which the reader can correct for himself in the light of the new formulations in Part Two.

18

For it seemed and seems to me of outstanding importance that the scheme for a new order in Germany came into being independently of the Hitler system and the present war, for it was and is the program of a young, active and growing political movement in the Reich. Not hatred of Hitler, nor the sourness of a refugee, nor a dread of military defeat, nor concessions to the western powers, guided my pen when I helped to draft that program. In 1930 none of those influences were at work — to say little of the fact that since then I have done my utmost to hinder such considerations from modifying my political thought and will.

This suffices to show that the plan for a new order in Germany issued from the sources of the German nature and of German history, and is therefore deeply based upon the national spirit, is essentially permanent — whereas dictatorship from without is nothing but a makeshift which every national wind can puff away. If, therefore, it should prove practicable to combine the safety of Europe with the reconstruction of Germany, then every true-hearted German nationalist must gladly accept the outcome.

This book is intended to provide the foundations for such a testing-time, penned by one who is convinced that German national security and European collaboration, far from being mutually exclusive, tend to favour one another.

OTTO STRASSER

Penned in Exile
*Easter 1940*

S REVOLUTION IN GER
POSSIBLE?

# IS REVOLUTION IN GERMANY POSSIBLE?

THE revolutionary character of the general situation in Germany is unquestionable. Indeed, the foundation of the historical and political views that have guided the thoughts and actions of myself and my friends is the fact that revolution has been going on in Germany for the last twenty years — a revolution of which the Hitler System is but one phase, the phase of destruction.

The caption of this Part One of my book can, therefore, relate only to the tactical question whether revolution is possible within the framework of the German Revolution at large, to the question whether the Hitler System can be overthrown, thereby initiating the last phase of the German Revolution. That phase will consist of the establishment of a new order.

Since the question 'Can the Hitler System be overthrown by an internal movement in Germany?' is thus tactical, it follows that the answer must likewise be mainly determined by tactical considerations. Such events as Hitler's striking successes in Scandinavia and the Balkans (successes indirectly due to his ally Stalin's victory in Finland) have a great influence upon the most immediate general outlooks, and are of decisive importance as regards the factor of time.

Having made this proviso, which must constantly be borne in mind, we discover that the following general features will help us to answer the question under discussion:

(1) The prevailing atmosphere, by which I mean the masses' widespread dissatisfaction with the present regime — a dissatisfaction for which (as usual) numerous, and often conflicting, causes can be found.

(2) The existence of a minority of persons prepared to take action, a minority willing and able at the appropriate moment to transform passive discontent into political action, much as a spark occurs to discharge electrical tensions that have accumulated beyond a certain amount.

(3) A paralysis of will within the system, or, rather, a paralysis of will among the active defenders of the system, because their self-confidence has been undermined, because their assurance of victory has waned, because they have lost discipline and resolution. In other words, for revolution to be possible a considerable number of those who wield the forces of the dominant system must have come to sympathize with the aims of the revolutionists, or must at least have ceased active opposition to these aims.

If we proceed to enquire how far, in the Germany of 1940, these fundamental prerequisites of a revolution exist, it can be unambiguously shown that the general atmosphere discloses all the features which make revolution possible.

So widespread, so virulent is the discontent of the German people with the dominant Hitler System (varying, of course, with the successes or failures of the system) that the enumeration of proofs would almost be superfluous. All the same, I shall give a summary of them, to avert the danger of that self-deception which makes dispassionateness impossible.

24

Surely one of the most convincing proofs is the fact that the Hitler System, after being in power for seven years, must still rely upon the detestable terrorist methods of the Gestapo and the concentration camps? Hereby Goebbels' chatter about 'popular support' of the Nazi regime is as flatly contradicted as by the ever more extensive gagging of the press, the wireless, and any other means by which the opinions of the German people seek expression.

Precise investigations have shown that the number of Germans who have pined for a longer or shorter time in concentration camps, penitentiaries, and prisons during the seven years of the Hitler regime totals more than two millions. Official statistics show, then, that over ten million Germans (if we add the dependents of the victims) have been so actively antagonistic to Hitler as to make personal acquaintance with his penal system. Nay more, many, many thousands of Germans have been put to death by their rulers, or, let us say bluntly, have been murdered.

Today these facts should be all the more emphatically proclaimed because they show, not only the profound hatred of the German people for the Hitler System, but also that an enormous part of the German people was actively fighting that system at a time when the foreign world was still associating with Hitler on friendly terms. What this signifies is that the same enormous part of the German people stands in the present 'European Civil War' on the side of Europe against the dictatorship of Hitler and Stalin, thus representing, not only a latent revolutionary force, but also a direct military force — inasmuch as the majority of the two million Germans

25

who are or have been under the Hitlerian harrow are
Germans of military age.

Less manifest but not less effective than the open
antagonism of the victims past and present in Hitler's
concentration camps, penitentiaries, and prisons, is the
voiceless discontent of the millions of those who are
apathetic in political matters. Among these, who consist
in very large measure of women, it is not so much
political or philosophical considerations which bring
them into opposition with the system, as the experiences
of daily life. The luxury of the Hitler bosses, the increasing brutalization of youth, the fall in real wages, the rise
in prices (which largely takes the form of a deterioration
in quality), the more and more oppressive demands
enforced upon the manual workers and anyone else
willing to make sacrifices, the mendacity of propaganda,
the alarming effects of the reign of terror, religious persecution, etc., were already operative before the war to
intensify discontent with the system among those who are
apathetic in politics and constitute something like 70%
of every nation. Hitler and Goebbels knew this just as
well as Himmler and Goering. But whereas the two
latter believed that the difficulty could be overcome by
tightening up the screw-press of the terror, the two former
were shrewd enough, in accordance with the old Roman
principle of 'bread and circuses', to replace the lacking
bread (read 'butter') by an abundance of circuses (read
'spectacular successes').

This made it essential for Hitler to gain spectacular
national successes, and the statesmen of the West were
too dull-witted to perceive that every time Hitler made
a coup on or across the frontier — as by his military

occupation of the Rhineland, his march into Austria, his conquest of Sudetenland, his annexation of Bohemia and Moravia, and his regaining of Memel — this was also a slap in the face for the opposition on the home front, made possible only by foreign aid. Each national success secured temporarily for Hitler the approval of the apathetic masses, who considered it a proof of 'the Leader's genius', and a reward to themselves for the sacrifices they were making.

But since the outbreak of war this stimulus has lost its savour, for the coming of war gave the lie to the piping of Goebbels during the last few years, to the unceasing declaration that 'the Leader will do it all without war'. During the first six or eight weeks after the declaration, the Germans were, in fact, panic-stricken. Then came recovery, thanks to the prompt victories in Poland, and the inertia of the western powers, especially as concerned their airforces. Still, the recovery of morale has by no means been complete, as would be shown speedily enough were Berlin to be bombarded from the skies.

Even though the dread of open belligerency that prevailed in Germany before the war has by now in great measure been appeased, the widespread discontent of the non-political masses has been greatly enhanced by the direct and indirect consequences of the blockade. Above all, women as thrifty housewives and as anxious mothers have been gravely discomfited by the scarcity of essential articles of diet, of footwear, and of clothing; and the daily expenditure of time and strength requisite for the attempt to satisfy these needs is both exhausting and discouraging. The consolations offered them by the obese Goering sound derisory, while dread of Himmler's

Gestapo will not prevent women's tongues from wagging while they stand for hours in queues, any more than it will prevent their whispering to one another about secret sources of 'black' supplies.

But what gets to work most powerfully among the Germans who are politically apathetic, what makes them Hitler's most dangerous enemies, is their remembrance of the last war. The increasing privations of 1917 and 1918 are the nightmares of the German women of 1939 and 1940, while the men meditate on the horrors of inflation, which robbed them of wages, savings, and profits, without a chance of defence. Neither proclamations nor bullying nor promises counteract these memories, for there was no lack of them twenty years ago, and little good did they do. Nor are the boastful reports of victories in Poland, of successes in the air, of the sinking of Allied ships by German submarines, any more effective. Every German who is over thirty knows full well that Ludendorff, likewise, conquered the whole of Poland, the whole of Serbia, the whole of Rumania, and that then Bulgaria and Turkey fought on Germany's side; every German over thirty knows how daily, weekly, and monthly the naval chiefs issued bulletins regarding the successes of the German submarines — successes that outdid even the victorious bulletins of Raeder and Goering — and that the end of it all were the Forest of Compiègne and the Hall of Mirrors at Versailles. Memories of these things (especially when they are vigorously exploited by an active propaganda) gives a political stamp today to the general discontent of the German people even when that discontent is not really the outcome of political causes.

Goebbels' declaration that 99 % of the German people are backing Hitler cannot be more strikingly disproved than by quoting the fact so incautiously divulged by the same propagandist concerning the famous vote taken among the inmates of Dachau concentration camp. They numbered 1572. Of these 1554 voted for Hitler, 8 against, while 10 abstained. Here you have your 99 % in favour of Hitler, but everyone knows what the 99 % of Dachauers were really thinking and feeling.

To sum up, then, we can be confident that the general atmosphere of dissatisfaction which is the first essential for every revolution undoubtedly exists today in the German people. The necessary stressing of the numerous, and for the most part non-political, causes of this discontent does not weaken its significance, since we are concerned only with a general atmosphere, and not with a lucid manifestation of the popular will.

This underlines the importance of the second of the three questions we set out to investigate in this connexion. Does there exist in Germany today a minority of persons willing and able to take action?

Of course we begin our answer by reminding ourselves of those who were Hitler's political adversaries before he seized power. Independents, majority socialists, democrats, centrists, 'People's Party' men, and German nationalists formed the patchwork front of those who from the end of 1918 to the end of 1932 shared responsibility for Germany's political life, and their representatives who were disqualified by Hitler therefore form the core of the German 'émigrés in the narrower sense of the term' (persons who, though they have not taken refuge abroad, may be assumed on principle to be opposed just as if they had fled).

To the left and to the right of those who were disqualified when Hitler seized power there were at that time the opposition groups, consisting of those who fought against Weimar just as they fought against Hitler — the Communists and the Black Front. The former were, or are, supporters of an international-Marxist-revolution; the latter were, or are, supporters of the German Revolution, that is to say of a new order in the sense of national freedom, social justice, and European collaboration.

In addition to these political groups of persons who oppose Hitler at home and abroad, there are the racial and religious groups of Hitler's adversaries: notably the Jews against whom Hitler and Streicher have preached a crusade; and the Catholic and Protestant Churches persecuted by Hitler and Rosenberg — in so far as they have not wholly or partially submitted. Of late, too, there has been what we may call a quasi-economic opposition, witnessed to by the flight of Edmund Stinnes to London, and even of Fritz Thyssen (who was a member of the Hitlerian Reichstag) to Switzerland.

The mere enumeration of these groups indicates how diversified are the trends, how varying the strength and the kind, of this multifarious oppositional movement against the Hitler System. Its extremely mixed composition is enough to show that no unified and vigorously acting community could possibly be formed out of it.

Speaking first of the 'dethroned Weimarians', their pugnacity diminishes as you pass among them from left to right. Even among the majority socialists there were

30

men of note, like Noske and Severing, who made peace with the Hitler System, while many other prominent members of this group became 'non-political'. Nevertheless it may be proclaimed that not only the party chiefs Wels and Vogel who became émigrés (taking refuge first in Prague and then in Paris), but also the steadfast old members of the party who stayed in Germany, continued firm opposition to the Hitler System, and that they could still rally many supporters from among the German working class.

The centrist Catholics proved less reliable, and still less reliable the bourgeois democrats. Almost all their leaders made peace with Hitler, and even refugee politicians like Brüning, Wirth, and Koch took up an attitude of reserve which (since they had considerable influence in England and the U.S.) was indirectly favourable to the Hitler System. Not until the anti-Christian policy of the Hitlerians became more marked, was a stronger opposition carried on from the Catholic side, but it never became distinctively political.

The same considerations apply more markedly to the 'People's Party' and German nationalist opposition, which was chiefly represented abroad by Treviranus, an ex-minister of the Reich. (There is a creditable exception, Dr. Rauschning, a German nationalist who was at one time president of the Danzig Senate.)

This brief sketch of the opposition formed by the various parties of the Weimar Republic makes it plain that only the social democrats were capable of producing a minority 'able and willing to take action' against the Hitler System; whereas the opposition formed by the other groups (individual exceptions apart) could do no more than intensify the general dissatisfaction; but was, even so, of considerable importance, especially in the religious sphere.

Fundamentally different, that is to say pugnacious, are the two opposition groups that stood on the left and right flanks of the old party opposition to the National Socialists, namely the Communists and the Black Front. In structure they were of a much more revolutionary type than the old legalist or constitutional party apparatus, and furthermore by their struggles in the pre-Hitler period had been better prepared for the new fighting conditions of illegality.

There can be no doubt that down to the outbreak of the war the Communists formed an opposition to the Hitler System, an opposition that was not always very adroit and consistent, but was absolutely uncompromising. If nevertheless they had no striking success, this is partly because since 1920-1921 the German people had inwardly outgrown the Communist peril; partly because the dictatorship of the Browns did not encourage a yearning for the dictatorship of the Reds, but rather favoured a desire for democratic freedom and self-government.

How much justification there was for the ingrained prejudice of the German people against the Communists was shown by the Hitler-Stalin pact, which gave outward expression to the internal kinship between the two systems.

With the formation of the Stalin-Hitler alliance the Communists were done for in Germany, both in their influence upon the German people and in the number of their membership. Inasmuch as every Communist both at home and abroad was transformed from an enemy of Hitler into an ally of Hitler, the German people (the industrial workers not excepted) ceased to draw a distinction between Communist and Hitlerian.

Since then, Communism in Germany has no longer been part of the opposition to Hitler, and this, perhaps, is the most satisfactory result of the Hitler-Stalin pact. For just as in foreign policy the clear line of the European struggle and still more of European reconstruction would have been blurred if Bolshevik Russia had continued to play a part in the democratic camp, so in home policy it would have been a misfortune had Communism been able to assert its claims as part of the German opposition to Hitler.

As concerns the Black Front, of which I am the leader, it has not only the tactical advantage of an organization which was from the first designed for secret (='black') work, but has also the advantage from the outlook of principle of having never taken part in the failures of the Weimar period. Still more important was the fact that it accurately foresaw and foretold the development of the Hitler System, with the result that its early members were strengthened in their convictions, and new recruits were steadily gained. Sufficient proof of this is given by the first January issue in 1937 of the Black Front organ known as 'Die Deutsche Revolution', of whose contents a full translation will be found in the Appendix to the present work (see below, p. 229). Since then the members of the Black Front in the Reich have been fortified by the evolution that has taken place in the interim. Of course this has not only increased their confidence, but has also promoted their influence on the surrounding strata of the population. The last notable point is the unique position of the Black Front in relation to the party and to the army — a matter about which there will be more to say in Part Two.

I cannot conclude this discussion of 'the minority of persons willing to take action' without considering the position of the army, which has a special part to play in the Hitler System. For a long time the hopes of foreign adversaries of Hitler (bourgeois for the most part) were concentrated upon the army, and they based these hopes upon what happened on June 30, 1934.

But they overlooked what I had set forth five years ago in my book *Die deutsche Bartholomäusnacht* [The German Massacre of St. Bartholomew] that on this very day Hitler had decided for what the generals wanted — namely for the war against the revolution. Subsequently the union between Hitler and the generals became closer and closer: Hitler complied with his allies' extravagant demands for armaments, and in the end even agreed to the pact with Russia they had unceasingly clamoured for, asking no more in return than that they should be loyal to his person and his system. When, on February 4, 1938, the remaining members of the general staff who had independent characters (above all, Generals Fritsch and Beck) were dismissed, this loyalty was ensured, and the 'Reichswehr Myth' had achieved its purpose.

It need hardly be said that this does not mean identity of views and aims between Hitler and the general staff. The grave internal and external dissensions between army and party persist, over and above the inevitable rivalry. Anyone acquainted with Prussian generals know that their egoism exceeds their loyalty. They would

34

not dream of allowing themselves to be dragged down to destruction with Hitler, and if Hitler's ruin were imminent they would seize any chance of saving themselves by the sacrifice of the Chancellor and his paladins. But this has nothing to do with opposition; it only means that the generals are unprincipled.

Since Hitler's purge of the general staff to rid it of men of character, there is, so far as concerns our search for a minority of persons 'willing and able to take action' in Germany, no dependence to be placed upon the leaders of the armed forces of the Reich. But it is otherwise as regards the commissioned officers of medium grade, especially in the army (for there is less to be said about the airforce and the navy). In these army circles not only does the best tradition of the German officers' corps remain active, but politically as well the ideas of the 'Schleicher School' still prevail — a school in which thousands of captains and majors were trained in youth. Among them there is, on principle, strong opposition to the Hitler System, while they cherish bitter memories of the murder of their leaders Schleicher and Bredow. It would be inexpedient to say much about this just now, but there can be no doubt as to the facts. Whereas the generals of the German army are an unprincipled lot, and the subalterns are ambitious youngsters who are politically apathetic or even devoted to Hitler — the majority of the staff officers are persons of blameless character, and in political matters are convinced as well as actively disposed opponents of the Hitler System.

To summarize the results of our search for 'a minority of persons willing and able to take action' against the Hitler System, we have found that such a minority really exists in the German nation, but still lacks unity of organization and purpose. It comprises three groups, the socialist group, the Black Front group, and the army group. In a word, it represents the Leipart-Strasser-Schleicher constellation which once before (in December 1932) was a deadly peril to Hitler. If it should prove practicable to bring these three groups into accord on the lines of the Schleicher-Strasser-Leipart combination, the anti-Hitler revolution would have a good chance of success.

The last stage of our study of the fundamental pre-requisites for a successful revolution against the Hitler System brings us to more concrete elements, the active defenders of that system; to the question whether a paralysis of will is likely among them. Who are they, these active defenders? In the narrower sense they are the army, the S.S. (Storm Guards), and the S.A. (Storm Troops), in the wider sense they are the whole National-Socialist Party and its members.

As regards the army, the foregoing disquisition has already solved a considerable part of our problem. Within the army there are strong and influential forces which are not merely untrustworthy from the outlook of upholders of the system, but are convinced opponents, and ready to take action. They will take action as soon as they are convinced that Hitler has become a danger to the national existence of Germany. A glance at the three-year-old Black Front periodical (see Appendix) will disclose the problem that faces every German officer and every German ranker with a sense of national responsibility — the problem of, Hitler or Germany?

(Appendix, p. 232). There is no decent ranker, there is no decent officer, who would not answer 'Germany' if he could only grasp the national necessity for a decision.

Himmler is well aware of this. The reports of thousands of spies who act as orderlies in the officers' mess-rooms have informed him of the spirit that is afoot — a spirit he fights in all possible ways. Everyone in the German army knows of the 'skirt' method he used so successfully in the cases of Blomberg and Brauchitsch; and also of the homosexual method he tried against Fritsch — but unavailingly, so that later he was compelled to have recourse to the time-honoured plan of assassination.

Exceedingly symptomatic was the speech upon *The Home Front in Germany* which he made to the officers' corps in the summer of 1937, whose wording shows much more plainly than does that of countless newspaper and magazine articles by refugees both Himmler's dread of the armed forces of the Reich and the Hitler System's dread of an internal revolution.

For defence, Himmler relies upon the police, the Gestapo, and especially upon the S.S., the Storm Guards and their 'Death's-Head Battalions'. Let me give a word-for-word extract from the aforesaid speech:

'Should war break out, I shall have the following tasks to perform. In view of what I consider to be the duties of the police, 15,000 men, or not more than 20,000 at the outside, will be withdrawn for service with the colours. The present total force of uniformed police is from 80,000 to 90,000. We have to remember that the great majority of these uniformed police consists of men who are over forty-five, or let us say over forty years of age, and therefore if I allow from 15,000 to 20,000 of the younger men to go to the army, I shall be parting with the steel of my police. In case of need I can replace them by calling back to active police duties men over fifty-five or over sixty.

'This will only be practical if I can make sure of an inner "stiffening" to be used for big and important actions. It will consist of the "Death's-Head Battalions".

'I shall be able to get along with my elderly policemen. The civilians over forty-five years of age who will be called up for auxiliary police service will, as has been arranged, carry out the duties that used to be assigned to the Landsturm. They will be able to do sentry-go at munition factories, railway-bridges, etc. — always providing that I have some younger men as "stiffening". These will be men between the ages of twenty-five and thirty-five belonging to the "Death's-Head Battalions" not older and not younger. I don't want very young men, or men who are well up in years, for the "sabotage-troops" and the "terror-troops" will consist of lively young fellows with up-to-date weapons — and I shall never be able to fight them with elderly Landsturmers.

'The "Death's-Head Battalions" will be stationed in every governmental district throughout Germany. They will be disposed of as follows:

'1. No Battalion will be stationed in its own native district. For instance, a Pomeranian Battalion will never serve in Pomerania.

'2. Each Battalion will be transferred to a new district every three weeks.

'3. No Battalion will be given street duty with its members isolated. It would never do for a man wearing the death's-head emblem to be stationed alone in the streets.

'4. This force will act ruthlessly. That is what it will be for.'

There can be no doubt that the Storm Guard Battalions, living in barracks, will fulfil their chief's hopes and will act ruthlessly towards their own nationals. But there is likely to be a hitch here in the case of Storm Guard Battalions not quartered in barracks. (This applies to nearly four-fifths of the total force of 300,000 men, for not more than 80,000 are kept in barracks.) They are simply working men, townsmen, and peasants — part of the people, and subject therefore to the popular mood.

This applies even more to the S.A., the Storm Troops. Numbering millions, they enjoy few of the advantages granted to the S.S., the Storm Guards; they are not to serve on the foreign front, but only on the 'home front'; this suffices to place them among the field-grey masses and estranges them from the Brown Shirts — let alone that it increases the long-standing friction between the S.S. (Storm Guards) and the S.A. (Storm Troops).

Even more decisive is the fact that comparatively few of the Storm Troopers are among the 'profiteers' of the system. On the contrary, they have for years been deceived and betrayed — especially since June 30, 1934. Immediately after the alleged attempt on Hitler's life in 1939, I got hold of a letter penned by one of the chiefs of the Storm Troopers, which contains the following passage (quoted verbatim):

'Various recent happenings have pleased me very much, although they have left a bitter taste in the mouth. All the same, with regard to the candidate for death I

39

hold Schiller's view, "The man must be helped". Un-fortunately, like the rest of us in Germany, I am badly off for news. My wireless apparatus doesn't work very well, for it needs an overhaul; and as for the newspapers, they lie so glibly that when one reads them one hardly knows whether one is standing on one's head or one's heels. Nothing shows this better than all the hubbub about the unfortunate Elser. What is true that is said about him, and what false? Perhaps you can tell me, for I really don't know. Most of it, I expect, arises out of Goebbels' imagination. I could tell you a lot of fine things, were it not for technical difficulties. But to come to the main point, we shall have to work hard and bring off our coup as soon as possible. We must approach the goal quickly, for there will be little chance of establishing a revolutionary Germany after a long war.'

I am sure that such a mood is the rule rather than the exception among the Storm Troopers, and for years it has seemed to me of the utmost importance to 'poison the minds' of the Storm Troop leaders (here, likewise, the middle grades rather than the men at the very top) with the watchwords of the Black Front. During the years 1933-1938 our *Huttenbriefe* were sent by the million to all sections of the Storm Troops and the National Socialist Party. The specimen reprinted in the Appendix (p. 241) gives an excellent example of our propagandist method.

Especially in the Party (where Gregor Strasser and the protracted work of the Kampf-Verlag (Fighting Publications) have not been forgotten) such activities have been most fruitful, more particularly in the Labour Front and among the Hitler Youth organizations.

What we must do now is make it clear to the abundant

profit-seekers within the party that Hitler's chances are practically nil, so that they will best promote their own interest if they take time by the forelock and adjust themselves to coming events. This sort of propaganda would induce hundreds of thousands of members, especially among the officialdom, to draw aloof from the regime; and where we are dealing with the more stubborn it will be well to use a stronger tone, and even to employ threats of personal retaliation. With the average members of the National Socialist Party the well-tried lures and deterrents of sweets and floggings will prove even more effective than they do with the generality of mankind.

Having shown that the three essential requisites for an internal revolution do actually exist in Germany, I have therewith reached a point still to be discussed — the tactical necessaries for such a revolution.

For simplicity, in expounding the tactical necessaries I shall stick to the same classification used in considering the general features of the revolutionary possibility.

As concerns the mood that prevails among the German masses, we must use all possible means for diffusing among them a sound knowledge of the world situation. It is hard for a foreigner to conceive how vast a gulf yawns between the world situation as it actually is, and the world situation as it presents itself to the minds of the German people. After seven years of Hitlerian dictatorship and Goebbelsian propaganda, this impoverished nation, exhausted and isolated both materially and spiritually, has been deprived of the possibility of forming a sound judgment of its own. The antecedents of the outbreak of war, the violation of the Czechs, the atrocities in Poland, the betrayal of Finland, the comparative strength of Germany and the western powers — these things are all as unknown to the German people as are the yielding disposition of France during the years 1933-1939 and the peaceful temper of Chamberlain's government. The German people has absolutely no idea of the detestation with which the rest of the world contemplates the Germany of Adolf Hitler, nor yet of the moral, political, and economic isolation of the country, which in 1940 is a hundredfold greater than it was in 1914.

The principal aid to peace will be anything that will acquaint the Germans with these plain facts, with the facts and nothing else. Not until the German people knows the truth will its present dull dissatisfaction be transformed into an active political will.

Here, too, what are spoken of as the 'War Aims' of the western powers play a very important part. One of Hitler's chief endeavours has been and is to inculcate the legend that the western powers desire the 'annihilation of Germany', and that consequently, were it merely for the sake of self-preservation, Germans must rally round their leaders — that is to say round himself. 'We are all in the same boat,' such is the leading theme of Goebbels' propaganda at the present time; and herein he voices nothing but his dread that the Germans may come to realize how the precise opposite is true. Anyone who wants to help himself and Germany must aid in downing Hitler and flinging him overboard.

An intimate knowledge of my fellow-countrymen has taught me that millions of them today are suffering from a conflict between their moral duty and what they still regard as a national duty. Directly the western

42

powers avow as their essential war aims the reversal of the violent deeds wrongfully committed by Hitler, but declare that they have no desire to discriminate against or destroy Germany, that very moment there will be an end to the cleavage in the minds of millions upon millions of Germans, and they will tranquilly obey their consciences — against Hitler.

Of course we cannot expect them to undertake an active campaign forthwith. It is idle to ask a fettered prisoner to begin by overpowering his heavily armed warder, and it is unfair to blame him as guilty because he is powerless. What we can demand of the German people, and what we forerunners among the champions of the German Revolution do demand, is passive resistance. But this comprehensive notion must be inculcated in numberless separate preliminary writings, by those able to avail themselves of all possible chances of diffusing information.

We must not say (I am thinking of things that can best be said by Germans) to the German aviator, 'Refuse to obey orders', for in that case as things are at present he will simply be court-martialled and put to death. What we should say is: 'Drop your bomb near what you are aiming at, but don't register a hit. No one can prove that you could have hit. In that way you will help to overthrow Hitler and to save Germany.' We must not say to the German worker, 'Down tools', for he would only be sent to a concentration camp. What we should say is: 'Do your work slowly and badly, misunderstand orders, waste material — but make sure you will never be found out.' To the clerks and officials we must say: 'Make a muddle of what you do; pretend to be stupid or overworked; address letters, documents, parcels wrongly; falsify lists and specifications; be tardy and disagreeable in your relations with the public, cautious but stupid in your relations with your superiors — in a word, "throw grit into the bearings whenever you have a chance; and even though each man does only a little, the massed effect will be stupendous.' To business and professional men: 'Be backward with the authorities, ask the revenue officials question after question, humbug customers while never forgetting to praise the Leader; remind them how Goering said, "Guns are more important than butter", delay the delivery of stamps on the ground that you are overworked, make complaint after complaint; all this will help to overthrow Hitler and therewith restore peace to Germany and Europe.'

I wrote simply, 'We must say'. Who are 'we', and how can we say it?

'We' are Germans who live free and can take up the fight against Hitler. I have enumerated the various groups of such persons. The outstanding personalities among them have a great moral and political responsibility — to their supporters, to the German people, and to the world at large. It speaks ill for them that they have not yet succeeded in forming a representative assembly of the German adversaries of Hitler. An impulse in the direction of establishing in foreign parts such a centralized representative body of Germans would act more quickly and effectively than anything else towards aggregating into united hopes for the future the moods of those malcontents who are scattered throughout the Reich, and towards concentrating the efforts of various groups in the minority that would gladly take action against the Hitler System. Nor could anything be more momentous than this in its influence upon the foreign world, whose cooperation will be indispensable to the speedy outbreak of a revolution against Hitler.

Again, 'how can we say it?' Uninfluential refugees, grudgingly tolerated as aliens, having no passports, no wireless stations, no funds to spare for direct and indirect propaganda, and persons to be numbered only by tens of thousands — how can we, actively disposed though we are, get in touch with the passive German masses, who are millions upon millions?

Apart from this problem, it is obviously our duty to do our utmost towards ending this war as soon as possible, towards ending it before its full powers of destruction have been wreaked. There can be no doubt that our only way of helping here is to promote the internal revolution against Hitler. The outcome of this preliminary investigation having been that such a revolution is possible, surely it behoves us to use all available means in order to bring it about? Such a question can only be answered in the affirmative. Three years ago Himmler emphasized the importance of *The Home Front in Germany*, and concluded his address to the officers' corps with the words of warning:

'An understanding that a completely new type of organization is essential must be universally diffused; so must the idea of the home front in Germany, upon the defence of which the very existence of the German nation will depend if we ever have to bear the burdens of war.'

It is time for the non-German world to understand Himmler's cry of distress and turn it to account.

45

Our enquiry is finished. Its upshot has been that as far as the objective requisites in Germany are concerned an internal revolution against Hitler is possible, but that there are indispensable subjective requisites as well.

To the foregoing disquisitions I must add one important remark: the trigger will be pulled by a military failure on Hitler's part.

For years in his foreign policy Hitler has scored triumph after triumph; even in the present war the military victories have, so far, all been Hitler's (in Poland) — with the result that up to now the word remains with him should the question of negotiations arise. While this state of affairs lasts, even the best propaganda and the most skilful underground work can only pave the way, generate doubt, undermine support, induce readiness to secede or to resist.

Not until the nimbus of victory has faded on Hitler's brow, not until his 'battle of the Marne' has convinced every German patriot that the alternative 'Hitler or Germany' has been presented, not until the military pre-eminence of the western powers becomes as plain as their moral superiority already is — not until then will the ice break that now encrusts the brains, the hearts, and the arms of the Germans.

That day will come, and will be followed by the day of the German Revolution which is enshrined as an object of ardent desire within the hearts of the German people.

Let us all be ready then, that our thoughts may be great, our wills pure, and our deeds just — for thereby only will storm-tossed and tormented humanity be enabled to reach the passionately desired goal of peace.

## PART TWO

IQUIDATION OF THE

ACE PROPOSALS OF TOMOF
GERMANY

# CHAPTER ONE

# PEACE OR ARMISTICE?

## 1. SIGNIFICANCE OF THE PEACE TREATY

No thoughtful person can fail to be aware that the present war, generated by the very nature and by the will of the Hitler System, will be decisive as to the future political, economic, and cultural order of Europe.

Germany itself, Austria, Czechoslovakia, and Poland give a heartbreaking picture of what this 'order' will be like should Hitler gain the victory.

What will that order be like should the Allies be victorious? We have no picture of it, unless we adopt the fatuous notion that it will be set up in utter forgetfulness of the twenty-five years between 1914 and 1939, that there will be re-established those pre-war conditions whose impracticability could not be better demonstrated than by the events of the two and a half decades that have followed the outbreak of the last great war.

Anyone who is convinced, as I am, that all historical happenings mean something, are the expression of a living development, will regard such reactionary ideas as incredible, and will pay no heed to them when discussing the political future.

If so, however, it becomes still more urgent to enquire what will be the nature of the new order to be established by the peace that will itself be the expression of the coming order.

For here we impinge upon the first question to present

itself at the close of every war. Shall we really try to make peace, true peace; or shall we be content with an armistice which, while ending the present war, will bear in its womb the embryo of a new one?

It is hard to raise such a question while war is still being waged; for the mere question may readily arouse dissensions within every belligerent power, and thus reduce the energy requisite for carrying the war to a successful conclusion. Since, however, experience teaches that it is even harder, much harder, to settle such a question properly when one side has gained a decisive victory, for in these circumstances the heat of passion so readily obscures the light of reason as well as the sense of justice, it is really incumbent on us, while we go on fighting, to prepare for peace, for the true peace that will make the recurrence of our present woes impossible.

But is a true peace possible? Can there truly be 'peace on earth'? Sceptics will be inclined to answer much as one who plays a leading part in this war answered me when I put the question that forms the title of this chapter: 'Are you fighting for a peace, or only for an armistice?' His reply was: 'What do you suppose? Every peace is nothing more than an armistice. The more difficult the peace, the longer will be the pause before the next war.'

Since I consider that the teachings of history dictate to us the laws of politics, I could not but agree, for the question was too general in its terms.

But if the question be put more concretely, in the form, 'Is durable peace possible in Europe?' I should answer, once more guided by the teachings of history, with an emphatic 'Yes'.

## 2. ELEMENTS OF EUROPEAN PEACE

At bottom what are wars but the struggles of growth among the nations? As soon as the peoples of a particular family of peoples within a particular area have finished growing, there cease between these peoples in this particular area the crises that result from the way in which growth has made them elbow one another, just as the cessation of feuds among the tribes and the clans established peace in the national units we now call Spain, Italy, France, Great Britain, Germany, etc. The end of the century-old struggle within these nations was a sign of the ripening of the characters or the personalities of these ripened nations, of the end of their 'becoming' stage. This was the necessary antecedent of the settlement that will finish the 'international' quarrels within the family of European nations.

Who can deny that all the nations of Europe, whether large or small, have entered the ripening phase of nationhood? Where can you find the Czech who wants to become a German; the Pole who wants to become a Russian; the Bulgarian who wants to become a Rumanian; or the Croat who wants to become a Serb — to say nothing of the nations that ripened yet earlier? Now the close of this ripening process necessarily involves our putting an end to any sort of intra-European imperialism — thus making both possible and indispensable a collaboration on the basis of the unconditional recognition of the freedom and independence of all the national 'personalities' which today comprise the European family.

Is not the remarkable lack of hatred in this war an indirect proof that the European nations feel themselves to belong to one family? Is not the talk about war aims that goes on simultaneously in the countries of all the belligerents a sign that, despite the struggle that continues, they have a yearning for community? Even Hitler and Goebbels feel impelled to declare that their only war aim is 'defence of Germany's right to live'; even they have to hide their imperialist actions behind a cloud of peaceful words, and to deck out the attack upon Europe they are delivering in concert with Stalin as a phase in the birth of Europe.

Have not the governments of the western powers also officially declared their war aim to be 'no territorial conquests, but a guarantee of security'; and is not this declaration a proof that those who take the lead in Britain and France have deduced the consequences of the completion of the ripening process among the nations of Europe and are determined to build thereon the coming peace?

But if this is so, we have no reason to fear that the coming peace will be nothing more than an armistice, and therefore it behoves us Germans to give the material and ideal guarantees of the security to which all the European nations are unconditionally entitled.

The central problem of the coming peace negotiations may therefore be stated thus:

How shall we combine the right to live of the German people who inhabit the centre of Europe, with other Europeans' need for security — and especially the need of the nations that adjoin Germany, the nations whose right to live is independent of what may happen to be their size?

## 3. DISINTEGRATION OF GERMANY?

Our formulation of the central problem will command almost unanimous assent, but there will be differences now that we come to the solution.

It would be foolish to deny that the demand for the disintegration of Germany will automatically tend to be voiced more loudly by the Allies the more the war spreads and the longer it lasts.

Just because this is so obvious, and for those who would be guided only by feelings so justifiable a trend, I will avoid trying to answer it on moral grounds. I shall content myself with a sober political rejoinder, which runs: 'True, the annihilation of an adversary will make it quite certain that he will never want to fight you again, and will therefore ensure a lasting peace'. The best example that can be cited to illustrate this is the example of the destruction of Carthage at the close of the third Punic war. The Romans killed all the men and boys of Carthage, sold the Punic women and girls into slavery, and razed to the ground the buildings of the rival city; and they symbolized the permanency of the destruction by driving a plough over the desert where Carthage had formerly stood. History tells us that there were no more Punic wars.

If an adversary can be definitively destroyed, a victorious power will naturally ask whether this will not be the best way of guaranteeing the security of its own people. Certainly I can find no moral arguments against such a course, though I am strongly convinced that under the sign of the cross such arguments would carry far more weight than they did in the days of pagan Rome. From the practical point of view, it was quite possible to kill half of the remaining 100,000 to 120,000 inhabitants of unhappy Carthage, and to sell the remaining half into slavery. But how could that be done with 70,000,000 Germans? Physical extirpation is simply out of the question, even if it were to be considered the best way of establishing peace in Europe.

I need not trouble to prove that no man living has so crazy an idea as this when he contends that the disintegration of Germany might be the best possible way of guaranteeing the peace he hopes to see established. He does not dream of the bodily extermination of the Germans, but of the destruction, or at any rate the weakening of the political organization of the country — of the disintegration of the German State.

The disintegration (or partition) of Germany means here that the left bank of the Rhine shall be annexed by France, or shall become a puppet State under French control; that East Prussia, with Danzig, the Corridor, and parts of Silesia, shall become Polish; that Sudetenland shall go back to a restored Czechoslovakia; that Austria shall be assigned to the Habsburgs (preferably to be combined with Czechoslovakia and Hungary into a 'Danubian Federation'); and that the remnants of Germany shall become 'protectorates', if possible under the tutelage of the recalled princely houses: the aim of all this being the permanent political impotence of the German people, whose activities are to be restricted to intellectual culture, industry, and agrarian production.

I shall not attempt to deny that this scheme may appear most desirable to the French, who less than seventy years ago suffered from the savage onslaught of

54

the Germans; or to assert that it would seem too cruel in the eyes of the Czechoslovaks and the Poles, who have been afflicted even more cruelly by the terrorist methods of Hitler.

On the contrary, for years I myself and many other German patriots have dreaded that this grotesque scheme may some day be realized, and it is as German nationalists inspired by such a dread that we have, in great measure, been prompted to carry on our campaign against the Hitler System. Let me again refer the reader to the illicit Black Front periodical which was circulated by millions in the Reich at the beginning of 1937, and is reproduced verbatim in the present work (See Appendix, p. 229).

Once more I will answer with practical rather than with moral arguments, by asking whether such a disintegration of Germany would create and stabilize peace.

I frankly recognize the possibility of such a disintegration of Germany, and I know that with a conquered nation the victors can do what they please — for a time. But how long will it last?

A peace settlement which is not felt and thought to be just by the conquered, will endure only so long as the conquerors have, and use, force to sustain it.

First, then, would the German people feel and think such a disintegration of Germany to be 'just'? I do not believe that any man or any woman can honestly say 'Yes'. If there are persons who can believe that economic security and possibilities for cultural development could reconcile the Germans to political castration, then I am convinced that such persons are labouring under a profound delusion. Just because they have, as I say,

'ripened', all the nations in Europe — the German nation
not excepted — lay the utmost stress upon political freedom, which includes the possibility of independently
developing whatever form of national existence they may
prefer.

Perhaps after a crushing defeat, and after seven years'
hunger and bodily chastisement, the German people
might accept such peace terms without demur, but as
soon as their palsy was over, as soon as the will-to-live
became active once more, the will-to-freedom, the will-
to-independence, and the will-to-equal-rights would also
return, and every German, young or old, would regard a
fight for German liberty and German unity as his supreme
aim.

Would this be wrong-headed? Is there a Frenchman,
an Englishman, a Pole, or a Czech who would act
differently in a similar situation?

Never will the Germans accommodate themselves to
the disintegration of Germany, to the tearing of their
country to tatters. If such peace terms are enforced,
those who enforce them will have to reckon upon the
permanent hostility of the Germans.

What this means is that the victors will have to remain
perpetually under arms to hold the Germans down — nay
more, that they will have to pile up their own armaments
proportionally with the recovery of the German people
from the consequences of defeat.

It means, last not least, that the victors will have to
reckon with the fact that a nation of 70,000,000 living in
Central Europe will be ready, at any moment when there
is an uneasy international situation (a war in the Far
East, troubles in the Pacific, threats from Russia, or what

not), to join forces with the disturbers of the peace, hoping under the shadow of this new menace to carry on their own struggle for freedom.

These are not moral arguments, neither menaces nor hopes — they are facts, hard facts, reinforced by the lessons of history and by the study of national psychology. Some may try to dismiss them as trifling, but none can deny their existence.

What could the disintegration of Germany signify, really; but that such a 'liquidation' of the war would eternalize the heavily armed and tense condition of Europe? It would signify that the Germans would concentrate their energies on unsettling the settlement, and that the other nations would have to concentrate theirs on trying to maintain it.

Peace? That would not be peace, but an armistice filled with hatred, an armistice whose duration would be limited by the strain put upon the victors to keep adequately armed — a strain that would grow worse the longer the armistice lasted.

# CHAPTER TWO

# FEDERALIZATION OF GERMANY

## I. PARTITION OF PRUSSIA

AT this stage it becomes necessary to insist that with the rejection of the plan to disintegrate Germany there must be associated practical proposals and guarantees from Germany for the security of her neighbours. The other nations of Europe, having been alarmed by Germany's foreign policy of late, will make it their first and most urgent demand that their governments shall fulfil what has been their principal war aim — and it is essential that the German people should give the requisite pledges and guarantees, having recognized that its own future in Europe is dependent thereon.

Nor must any German statesman fail to understand that German utterances and promises, even when signed, sealed, and delivered, are now practically valueless on the international exchange. Too often have German governments, made up of no matter what persons, failed to keep their pledges, broken their oaths, and treated documents duly signed by them as no more than 'scraps of paper'. No clear-sighted German publicist will take it amiss if non-Germans now demand from Germans, not words, but deeds.

The most decisive of such deeds will be the partition of Prussia.

In view of the profuse outpouring of historical literature during the last great war, there is no need to adduce

58

detailed justification of this demand. Suffice it to say that as long ago as 1931 the Black Front endorsed the idea in its first public statement of aims, entitled *Aufbau des deutschen Sozialismus* [Structure of German Socialism], penned by myself (see below, pp. 117 and foll.); and that on September 20 of the same year, in No. 34 of its central organ 'Die Schwarze Front' (of which I was editor), it gave an exact description — with a map — of the proposed partition of Prussia, and of what was to be the territorial distribution of the New Germany.

Consequently the German demand for the partition of Prussia originated, not under the stresses of war, not because of fear of military defeat, not as the outcome of foreign or refugee influence — but owing to the overwhelming logic of a study of the political and religious structure of Germany, its history, and its motive forces, when contemplated by a European consciousness. I regard it as of the utmost importance to insist on this today.

No one well acquainted with the spirit of Germany can overlook the fact that for centuries within the German people there has been a mental and political struggle between what I have called the Frederician (the Prussian) and what I have called the Theresian (the Austrian) sections. This may be compared with the struggle that goes on in a child's mind between the paternal and the maternal elements — a struggle which, as character develops — ultimately leads to the formation of a (new) unity. The concept 'German' contains, and transcends, both the Frederician (Protestant) and the Theresian (Catholic) elements, wherein is mirrored all the multiplicity of the tribal souls that have respectively contributed to the over-riding concept 'German', without having, so far, completely merged their identity in it.

Considered from an evolutionary standpoint, 'Prussian' signifies the fateful domination of a partial element over the whole, and is analogous to what is seen in pathology when a cancer results from an excessive and boundless proliferation of certain local cells, that master (and destroy) the organism to which they belonged.

Politically, therefore, the development of Little Brandenburg into Great Prussia represents the growth of a cancer threatening the life of the German body as a whole, and it is a development which must be checked at all costs if Germany, and Europe, are to be saved. For it lies in the very nature of the doctrine 'might is right', a doctrine which forms the heart of the Prussian mystery, that it should know no limits. That was why Brandenburg grew into Prussia; Prussia into Great Prussia, which struts as Germany — in the belief that Great Prussia will grow into the Continental Empire that would like to strut as Europe.

We Germans must ourselves overcome Prussia. We must overcome it territorially, economically, and spiritually; for only when we have done so will New Germany, will New Europe, become possible.

## 2. FEDERATION OF THE PROVINCES

The fundamental principle of German organization is the federative principle, based upon the German tribes which have for ages been rooted in their respective territories, refusing to merge and willing only to federate.

The political structure of the millenniary German Reich

has been based upon this federative segmentation, upon the voluntary collaboration of all the tribes, upon the organic union of its territories.

This teaching of a great past was rendered inaudible by the clamour of Prussian propaganda. Force replaced voluntary collaboration. The various territories, instead of being given a chance to develop as they respectively wished, were compelled to 'toe the Prussian line'.

The territorial subdivision of Prussia must precede the federalization of Germany, whose territories (like the Swiss cantons) are tribal settlements, historical and economic units, which form voluntary collaborators in the German Reich.

Put more concretely, this signifies the re-establishment of the 'Landschaften' or provinces of Rhineland, Hesse, Hanover, Thuringia, Saxony, Brandenburg, etc., in place of what now constitutes Prussia; the re-establishment of the provinces of Swabia, Franconia, Bavaria, etc., in place of what now constitute Wurtemberg, Baden, Hohenzollern, Bavaria — in a word, the territorial subdivision of Germany into about fifteen provinces representing political, cultural, tribal, and economic units.

These provinces, having on the average not more than about five million inhabitants each, would enjoy rights of local self-government rather more extensive than those of the Swiss cantons. As do the cantons, each province would control its own government and its own popular assembly; and (this is most important) all its functionaries, from president to postman, would be natives of that particular territory. The aim should even be to make sure that the federal officials assigned to any province should as far as possible be natives of that province.

The territorial disintegration of Prussia would thus be supplemented by the destruction of the extant centralized administrative apparatus which is one of the most powerful weapons of Prussian power politics. This would be replaced by the federal administrative apparatus of the respective provinces, which in its turn would be localized, with the greatest possible amount of self-government and democratic State-control.

The 'German Reich' would thus veritably become a league of substantially independent cantons, whose joint instruments, the federal government and the popular assembly, would be reinforced and controlled by the body of provincial presidents. It may be taken as a matter of course that Berlin would cease to be the capital of the Reich. I myself think there is a good deal to be said in favour of Ratisbon.

The details of the political structure of New Germany will be considered in Part Three of this book.

Suffice it for the moment to insist that the destruction of Prussia, the reconstitution of the provinces which during the last century and a half have, one after another, been 'gobbled up' by Prussia, the subdivision of Germany into a league of federative provinces, are to be regarded as indispensable preliminaries to the upbuilding of New Germany.

It is heart-rending today to read an account of the disputes between the Allied statesmen and those of Germany that followed the surrender of November 1918. An utter lack of psychological and historical knowledge on the part of the former was supplemented by the stupidity and weakness of the latter, with the result that behind the mask of the Weimar Republic to begin with, and behind the mask of Hindenburg and Hitler subsequently, the power of Prussia became firmly re-established, to resume the lost game after the lapse of twenty-one years.

If those who will be responsible for the peace that will some day follow this war want to put an end to the game for ever, they must remember that there is only one way of doing so:

Not by the disintegration of Germany, but by the partition of Prussia.

## 3. SOCIAL RECONSTRUCTION

The demand for the 'partition of Prussia' would be not more than half complied with if the term were to mean only a territorial subdivision and the destruction of the centralized administrative apparatus.

The roots of Prussian power are quite as much social, economic, and psychological; and without the destruction of these roots it will avail little to divide the stalks and pluck the leaves, or even to pick the fruit.

The social power of Prussia is based upon the squire-archy, the power of the junkers. These, numbering 18,688, own 16.7 % of the land used in Prussia for agriculture and stock-raising. This is more than one-quarter of the land so farmed, the rest being farmed by the small-holders, the peasants who comprise 4,500,000. The feudalist caste of the Prussian junkers, the big landowners, form the pillars of the Prussian State, Prussian militarism, and Prussian power politics.

Without the social and economic overthrow of the junker caste, without depriving the Prussian junkers of their power, there can be no lasting partition of Prussia, and therefore no New Germany.

Far be it from me (a conservative as well as a revolutionist) to deny the strength, the value, and the significance of this sustaining stratum for the origin and existence of Prussia, and — during a certain phase — of Germany no less. Every people needs a sustaining stratum, and no one but an intellectual out of touch with the actualities of life can fail to see the notable part that has been played by the aristocracy as the sustaining stratum of the nation.

But every sustaining stratum, every aristrocracy, must comply with the demands of the time. The French noblesse was slower to recognize this than the English gentry had been, and that was why the French noblesse fell before Danton's revolution, whereas the English gentry survived Cromwell's revolution. The Prussian junker caste does not understand the situation in the least. Neither in 1918 nor in 1933 did it hear the call of the time, but hid as pusillanimously behind the mask of Hitler as it had hidden behind the mask of Ebert, caring only to keep its social and economic power and seizing any chance for carrying on its reactionary policy.

If, therefore, we wish to make an end of Prussianism, we must deal radically with these representatives of political reaction.

This means that the great estates will have to be divided up, and that monopolist industries must be nationalized.

For side by side with the Old Prussian estate of junkers or great landowners, there came into existence after the foundation of the Bismarckian Reich (which,

64

under the device of the Weimar Republic, transformed itself more and more into Great Prussia), the New Prussian estate of heavy industrials, represented towards the last by Krupp and Thyssen, much as the junkers were represented by Wangenheim and Oldenburg-Januschau.

It is possible, nay probable, that influential circles in England and France, having sympathy with the Prusso-German social strata that will be hit hard by such measures, will regard the plan as unduly revolutionary, not to say 'bolshevik'. The main argument here must be a political one. The sympathizers must be shown that unless we strike at the roots of the great landowners' and heavy industrialists' power, it will be impossible to make an end of Prussia and Prusso-German imperialism.

It will be necessary, however, to show that this expropriation is not to be effected without compensation, nor yet in favour of the State or of any kind of State socialism, but only in favour of self-governing economic corporations in the industrial domain. (This matter, likewise, will be more fully discussed in Part Three.)

My rejection on principle of any kind of bolshevism (and of the Marxism on which it is based), together with my insistence on the maintenance of individual rights, creative initiative, and the pursuit of economic gain, must protect me against an erroneous interpretation of my demand for the subdivision of great landed estates and the nationalization of monopolist industry.

Whoever recognizes the truth of the saying 'Property makes free', whoever affirms the necessity for a sustaining stratum in any satisfactory social order — must look forward to the new order which will aim at the deproletarianization of the people, and at our liberation from the social and economic monopolies under whose harrow no sort of freedom is possible.

## 4. DEMOCRACY OF THE VOCATIONAL ESTATES

The picture of the far-reaching structural transformation requisite to establish the New Germany (a transformation which would have taken place even without this war because it would have come as the completion of the revolutionary changes that have been going on since 1918) would be unfinished did it not disclose the fundamental democratization that is essential to intra-European collaboration.

For Wilson in 1918, and Chamberlain and Daladier in 1939, rightly insisted that the new condition of Europe, which must be and would be the outcome of the war, could only be lasting if it were based upon democratic freedom and self-government.

But when we say this, we must not forget Germany's experiences from 1918-1933 in the matter of what was called formal democracy; nor the way in which the western powers, under the pressure of the necessities of war, have been compelled to make many changes in the machinery of democratic government.

It must be added that in Germany since Hitler seized power it has become impossible to grant equal rights in any sense to the totalitarian parties of the Nazis or the Bolsheviks; and, on the other hand, that under the hitherto prevailing form of party democracy it would be impossible to refuse them these equal rights; and, finally, that the social and economic dethronement of what have heretofore been the leading strata must somehow be ensured under the future form of democracy (read 'popular government').

All these considerations join forces for the rejection of party democracy in the New Germany, and for the acceptance of the democracy of the vocational estates.

Those acquainted with the internal development of Germany may be glad to discern here the old ideas of the councils' system which in 1918-1919 the masses of the people vainly urged the petty-bourgeois social democratic leaders to work for. (From the first at that time the traditional forces of Prussian-Germany were powerfully operative among the petty-bourgeois social democratic leaders.)

Today, when the party of Hitlerism and Bolshevism numbers many millions, every keen observer of German conditions will agree that nothing but the elimination of all parties and the inauguration of a democracy of the councils and the estates can create the new form of democracy that is essential both for home and foreign affairs.

Once more I am only dealing here in outline with a matter that will be more fully discussed in Part Three of my book; and the fact that the program was drafted in the years 1930 and 1931 should convince my readers that the proposals were based upon the then situation of Germany, and have not arisen out of the actual position of the belligerents.

The basic maxim of this new form of democracy runs: self-government by the estates, and their direct control of the political administration.

There are two routes along which this goal will be reached: first by the construction of a comprehensive organization of persons engaged in all vocations, in five councils of manual workers, peasants, employees and officials, manufacturers and traders, and members of the liberal professions.

Secondly the people at large will secure its share of power through joint chambers of estates which will be set up in every district, every province, and last of all in the Reich, to become a determinative factor in administration and legislation.

This system of popular representation based upon direct and indirect elections, representing in the councils the economic interests and in the vocational estates the political popular interests, seems to be the only way of avoiding in Germany, not only any return of the reaction, but also any revival of the Nazi and Bolshevik party movements.

## 5. THE NEW SPIRIT

No political, social, and economic methods of organization would be of permanent value, unless this work were crowned by the deliberate inauguration and cultivation of a new spirit.

This spirit of the New Germany must and will be a repudiation of the belief that might and force should regulate the social life of mankind. There must and will be a recognition, both in substance and in form, that voluntary collaboration is to be the basis of human society.

Force or voluntary collaboration? — that is one of the

fundamental matters about which this war is being fought. The answer can only be collaboration, both national and international.

In Germany this new Spirit (which was as clearly foreshadowed by Herder, as the spirit of William II and Hitler was foreshadowed by Hegel) is most clearly manifested by the passionate repudiation of the idols of the totalitarian State, and by the whole-hearted acceptance of Christianity with its doctrines of the freedom and dignity of the human soul.

In defiance of the Old Prussian prophets of State-hegemony and the modern German advocates of race-hegemony, the spirit of the West proclaims the fathership of God and the sonship of man — of all men — and insists upon the dependence of all human institutions (the State not excepted) upon the Law of God.

We fully recognize that the polarity Emperor-Pope, State-Church, represents the very essence of Europe, which cannot be removed, cannot be dispensed with, without destroying the spirit and the soul of Europe.

Freedom of the spirit, of belief, of conscience, are the foundations of Europe, and New Germany would cut itself away from Europe should it fail to proclaim them and to respect them.

No less important as fundamentals of this European spirit of the New Germany, are the independence of the press, of science, and of art, which must be free from any sort of State interference or social monopolization.

Education and the school should have no other aims than to promote the development of free personalities, to foster the growth of frank and great souls. They will best do this by ensuring the unrestricted development of the divine soul, thanks to which each of us, after his kind and according to his powers, can fulfil himself, and thus sing the praises of the Creator who fashioned his soul as it is and no otherwise.

The diversity of human beings, the differences among them in quality and value, their varying powers and their varying tones, are intrinsic. All that education can achieve is to foster the beauty of the tones given out by each soul, so that when sounding together they can produce the harmony that will guarantee inward and outward peace.

## 6. RENUNCIATION OF MILITARISM

Such an avowal of a new spirit would be an idle declamation unless it had prompt political consequences.

For the New Germany, one of these decisive results would be the renunciation of Prussian militarism both on principle and as a form of organization.

Unquestionably in foreign parts the idea of Prussia was embodied, not so much in the knowledge of any philosophy she might proclaim, as in an experience of what use she made of her highly developed militarism. Her practice counted for more than her precept, were it only because of the sinister consequences of her practice.

In this connexion we must on no account forget to allow for two decisive facts: first of all that, as a famous historian has said, the nineteenth century was pre-eminently the age of imperialism, and therefore manifested a distinctive political structure that was by no means confined to Prussianized Germany; secondly that militarism had become a strange epidemic phenomenon, an epidemic malady of the now unbelieving souls of European human beings.

No less notable a man than Masaryk, a great statesman and philosopher (whose pupil I may take this opportunity of again declaring myself to be) recognized this phenomenon, and described it as follows:

'Modern militarism, especially Prussian militarism, is, considered scientifically and philosophically, a system of objectification — a panic flight on the part of morbid subjectivity and suicidal mania . . . When Sombart, in the Hegelian manner, extolled German militarism, and bragged about fighting in the trenches beside Faust and Zarathustra, he did not realize how he was condemning German and European civilization as drenched with blood. What else is the war-making of modern civilized human beings than a panic flight from the anxieties that arise in the 'ego' of the superman. That is why, as regards bellicosity, the intellectuals are as bad as, or worse than, the agriculturists and the urban workers. . . . Modern man suffers from a morbid suicidal impulse, from the fatigue and the anxiety that result from his spiritual and moral isolation. Militarism represents the superman's attempt to escape from this malady, which it really aggravates. In the nation of thinkers and philosophers there is the largest percentage of suicides; that nation has the most highly developed militarism, and it was mainly responsible for the world war.'

Masaryk had good reasons for emphasizing this characteristic feature of contemporary Europe; and he pointed out as the crowning 'sin' of Prussia that there the spiritual malady of modern Europeans had been promoted into an ideal and a system.

The German people, more subject than any other to this spiritual malady and suffering from it in its worst form, taking to heart Clemenceau's profound remark that the Germans' chief danger is their being in love with death, must do their utmost to seek a cure.

A radical and lasting cure can only come from a religious revival, can only come from their giving a new significance to life by internal freedom and devotion to Christianity.

Prussian militarism must be overcome; in the spiritual field by a new ideal of life, and in the practical field by a new military organization.

In the last section I mentioned the philosophical aims of education and the school. To these must be added the practical aim of drafting and exercising a new ideal of life. The hysterical heroism which has been adopted as the ideal of life in Hitlerian Germany, must be shown to be what it is, must be condemned and rejected as deceptive, as a swindle, as a denial of the truth of life.

The joy of life, the Song of Songs whose strophes must be unfailingly sung to an impoverished, proletarianized, mechanized, and nihilistic mankind, will be the best prophylactic of the epidemic disease of suicidal impulse and militarism. When people have grasped the fact that schools of cookery are much more important than schools of politics, and that the amount of laughter which can be heard is the best indication of the quality of their political and economic institutions, the spirit of militarism will have been definitively overcome.

But in practice it will most promptly be overcome by a change in the prevailing military system.

In accordance with my conviction of the diversity of human beings and of their right to self-determination, I hereby declare myself absolutely opposed to universal military service.

In the first program of the Black Front we demanded that army duty in Germany should be a voluntary affair; and this, not least, because thereby would be facilitated the new joint military system of a general European army such as a European Federation will need.

But if (and this will be one of the main topics of discussion at the coming Peace Conference) such a joint military system cannot yet be established by the United States of Europe, there will remain for our model the Swiss militia system, which maintains universal service, but wherein the origin of any form of militarism is rendered impracticable by the most carefully devised democratic safeguards.

Between the two possibilities, between a small professional army under European control and a militia army after the Swiss model, the New Germany will have to choose as the basis of its future military organization — of course in cooperation with the Peace Conference. Neither scheme would leave any scope for Prussian . militarism.

## 7. A WORD ON THE JEWISH PROBLEM

Theoretical and practical considerations make it expedient to add a few words about the problem which, since the rise of the Hitler System, has become a world-wide problem, and one whose settlement will be an urgent topic at the Peace Conference. I refer to the Jewish problem.

In various parts of my *Deutsche Revolution* and in numerous articles in the international press I have expressed the utmost disapproval of the shameless and inhuman anti-Jewish campaign that has characterized the Hitler System; and I may also mention that as early as 1928, in a party periodical, I protested editorially against antisemitism of the Streicher brand, voicing the war-cry, 'Antisemitism is dead. Long live the idea of the People!'

This advocacy of the idea of the People logically implied the disavowal of any valuation of peoples or nations as good or bad, as better or worse, since they all have equal rights, equal needs, and equal duties, in accordance with the will of the Creator, who gave each of them its own kind, its own nature, and its own tasks. This profound respect for organic life, and the fact that it is necessary for us and incumbent on us to recognize and maintain human dignity, imply that it will be an unconditional part of the social and political organization of New Germany to maintain the equal rights of all human beings.

Yet this fundamental principle of equality must not be considered to invalidate the organic law that the peoples and nations are fundamentally different, with the result that they urgently need differences in their social and political institutions — a fact which every government is bound to take into account.

In practical politics, therefore, there arises the problem of national minorities, whose relations to the national majorities in any area may present difficulties not local merely (as in Germany, for instance), but pertaining to Europe as a whole. Speaking generally it may be said that a comprehensive and just solution will only be possible within the framework of the European Federation, where the simultaneous interests of almost all the European peoples, whether as States or as national minorities, will ensure that whatever legal arrangements are made will be universally regarded as just, and will therefore be faithfully adhered to.

But since this desirable joint solution will need time to achieve, New Germany will have meanwhile to set to work by herself to solve the problem of national minorities (and therewith the Jewish problem) in that modern spirit which will pay due regard both to the organic laws of ethnical differences and to the moral laws according to which all human beings have equal rights. Politically considered there are three alternative solutions:

(1) Persons of different racial origin from the majority may be described as foreigners.

(2) Groups of persons of various racial stamps may be deemed to constitute national minorities.

(3) Persons belonging to different stocks may be incorporated into the main body of the nation by assimilation.

All three methods are equally possible and equally honourable, with the urgent proviso that every adult person of another stock than that of the majority must himself or herself have full right to decide which method to adopt.

As a matter of principle, there is no difference between the general treatment of the problem of national

75

minorities and the treatment of the Jewish problem. If the latter is separately considered here, this is because the peculiar way in which the question has presented itself makes separate consideration expedient.

I recommend the above tripartite approach to the matter as regards the Jews, because the formulation is not the outcome of any fine-spun theory, but is grounded upon the actual circumstances which must form the basis of any new settlement of the Jewish problem.

(1) The category of foreigners emerges from the fact that of late years there has been a widespread development of the movement known as Zionism, which should be supported by all 'nation-conscious' persons and peoples as a genuine endeavour for the renovation of Judaism.

(2) The category of national minorities corresponds to the political fact that European Jewry has been domiciled in Europe for many centuries, and in each country rightly regards itself as belonging to that country, though it does not wish to forsake its own national religion and its own national peculiarities.

(3) The category of assimilation is nevertheless (despite Hitler and his materialistic racial theory) a datum of the position of the Jews in Germany and the rest of Europe, in conformity with the accepted humanist doctrine that every human being is entitled to liberty and self-determination — a doctrine which New Germany will unhesitatingly accept. Although we do not deny our biological subordination to blood, race, and nationality, we must emphatically proclaim that the human spirit is privileged and competent to overcome this subordination, and, as knowledge and choice

may decide, to adopt the present and future views upon these matters.

It is likely enough that the preponderant majority of German Jews will prefer to belong to the Jewish commonwealth. Among these there will doubtless be many who in former days were antagonistic to Zionism, and perhaps even now are by no means wholly reconciled to it, but will lose their scruples when they become aware that as Jews, as members of the Jewish commonwealth, they can still remain united to Germany while preserving a Jewish stamp — inasmuch as the Jewish national group will be incorporated into New Germany. This very fact, their permanent incorporation into Germany, will distinguish them from the Jews, say, of Palestine or Poland — not in substance, but in many of the forms of life.

Of course this incorporation into Germany is fundamentally diverse from the complete assimilation that will occur in the case of those belonging to the third category. These latter will have to abandon Judaism as a national religion, and will have to give this and other guarantees of their determination to become Germans in every respect. (Consider here the demands which every modern State tends more and more to make of alien elements that are to be incorporated and fully assimilated.)

Of decisive importance as regards this question of the political treatment of minorities (including the Jews) is it that there should be established a State Department of National Minorities whose head must be a member of the government, and would automatically become the representative of the national minorities of his country in the League of Nations (and in due course in the European Federation). Inasmuch as he would naturally be chosen from the largest national minority, this minister of State would in Germany obviously be of Jewish blood — a fact which would indicate the soundness of the proposed solution, and would have an excellent effect both at home and abroad.

# CHAPTER THREE

# PROBLEMS OF THE PEACE CONFERENCE

## I. PRELIMINARIES TO PEACE

THE previous sections have been concerned with questions that will become urgent when the war is over, and the way in which these questions are answered will be decisive as to the kind and the duration of the peace that will ensue. They are questions that will primarily have to be solved by the Germans themselves. Their connexion with the present war lies mainly in this, that the war was in great measure launched by Hitler and his henchmen in order to frustrate the solution of these intra-German and economic problems.

But the world-public at large will not be so much exercised about intra-German problems as about problems that have to do with the relations between Germany and her neighbours. These latter are problems that have been raised by the war, and their discussion, before all, will be the topic of the peace negotiations.

Immediately, therefore, we reach the crux of the matter. Will the blunders of Versailles be avoided, or will they not?

The brilliant French historian, Jacques Bainville, whose work on the Treaty of Versailles [*Les conséquences politiques de la paix*, Paris, 1920] is today valued as a prophecy that has been fulfilled, joins the German critics of the peace conditions of 1919 — though for other reasons than the Germans. Whereas the Germans consider Versailles to have been unduly harsh, Bainville deems it too lenient — and both parties seem to have been justified by the results.

The fact was that the most urgent problems were then very little understood, so that those who had to solve them were not ready for their task. Old and new outlooks, superficial and profound discussions, sound and unsound methods, were grotesquely intermingled, with the unfortunate consequence that, far from reinforcing one another, they cancelled one another out.

The Peace of Versailles, like those dictated at Brest-Litovsk and Bucharest, was a nineteenth-century and not a twentieth-century peace. But the peace that follows the present war must give a new visage to twentieth-century Europe.

Without for a moment ignoring the material demands for general security which Germany will have to satisfy in order to atone for her complicity in Hitler's outburst of violence (an atonement whose effects will be more lasting, the more thorough and the more enduring the German repudiation of the Hitler System), the coming peace must be designed with an eye to the future of Europe, to averting the evils that stand in the way of the true pacification and the trusty collaboration of the peoples of our continent.

This peace must embody:

(1) The principle of liberty, of independence, of self-determination for all nations, large or small.

(2) The principle that right, not might, shall prevail

80

in all nations, both in their domestic and in their foreign affairs.

(3) The principle of joint security, joint wellbeing, and joint culture.

These same principles must likewise secure expression in the preliminaries to the peace, and in the methods by which it is approached.

On the German side an essential will be that the Germans must repudiate on principle Hitler's unwarrantable use of force, and the conditions that have resulted therefrom. Without such repudiation there can be neither armistice nor peace.

The repudiation of Hitler's unwarrantable use of force will imply the immediate evacuation by German troops of all the non-German areas they may have occupied, and a pledge to pay compensation for any damage they may have done.

This re-establishment of right as against might will not be a part of the peace, but a preliminary to peace, and a main constituent of the agreement for an armistice.

The peace itself, if it is to deserve that name, must not be the upshot of a dictatorship, but of comprehensive negotiations, not only between Germany and her adversaries, for the neutrals great and small must participate in them, probably choosing the United States and Italy as their representatives. A sort of Vienna Congress will have to debate and adjust the interests and wishes of the peoples of Europe, and elaborate a harmony, bearing ever in mind the great commonwealth of Europe and the salvation of the West.

## 2. THE GERMAN PARTNER

It becomes necessary here to consider a question which also involves matters of principle. Who will represent Germany at this Peace Conference?

Those who have read my book thus far will see plainly enough that it cannot be an envoy from a masked or modified Hitlerian government, nor yet from a 'government of generals', but must be someone despatched by the government of the German Revolution.

For a successful revolution against Hitler before the military collapse of Germany will not only be the decisive contribution of the German people to the cause of peace, but also the requisite proof of the genuineness and durability of a change in the political structure of the country.

Upon this will not only depend (for the most part) the readiness of the Allies to make a just peace; for nothing else can guarantee that the world has not to do with an act of despair on the part of the German people, or with an attempt at camouflage on the part of the Prussian militarist stratum, but that Germany is honestly animated by the constructive will to upbuild a New Germany and make a voluntary contribution to a New Europe.

If we do our best to ascertain what are the forces and the personalities that can be expected to make the German Revolution, and afterwards to represent Germany at the Peace Conference, we shall be glad to find that within Germany they are far stronger and more unified than is obvious or than people outside Germany suppose.

This depends mainly upon the fact that the political medley of those who comprise the mass of German refugees in foreign parts does not constitute a proper reflexion of the internal situation of Germany, or of what is taking place there.

The fact that thousands of human beings have fled from a region devastated by earthquake does not create any sort of spiritual unity among them. That is why to refugees, to those who were constituents of a political order that has been overthrown, there clings an odour of Coblenz [a rendezvous of émigrés during the French Revolution a century and a half ago]; why they always seem to be persons 'who have learned nothing and forgotten nothing'.

A few only of the German émigrés, who in mind at least have remained youthful, have had energy for self-knowledge, have been able to go on learning, so that they have been able to place themselves at the front of the coming German Revolution. Not all of them are working outside the frontiers of the Reich. Nor are they merely to be regarded as the vanquished of yesterday. They are the revolutionaries of tomorrow. They have fought, and continue fighting, not only against yesterday (the Weimar Republic), but against today (the Hitler System).

If, bearing these facts in mind, we study the forces of the German Revolution, we encounter a front which manifested itself several years ago in Germany, being then named after its most noted leaders the Schleicher-Strasser-Leipart Front.

Some of the high officers of the armed forces, consisting of Schleicher (the 'socialist general') and his intimates,

had, animated by a close acquaintance with the dangers
of the situation, broken with the junkers (when the
Eastern Aid scandal became notorious) and with the
great capitalists (Hugenberg and Thyssen), and made
successful advances to the revolutionary socialist youth,
whose spiritual leader was Möller van den Bruck and
whose chief organizer was Gregor Strasser. Together
they sought and found a way to the anti-bolshevik but
socialist workers who, led by Leipart, had ready in the
trade unions the foundation stones for a new future.

To the old powers of Prussianized Germany this
alliance of modern officers with the revolutionary youth
and the solid elements of the working-class seemed so
desperately dangerous that they were resolved at all
hazards to smash it; and Hindenburg, the Prussian, with
his whipper-in Oldenburg-Januschau, the junker, replaced the revolutionary group of Schleicher, Strasser,
and Leipart by the reactionary group of Papen, Hitler,
and Hugenberg — with the foreseen (and desired) result
that instead of an immediate internal revolution there
came, in due course, a war across the frontiers.

But the forces of the German Revolution which then,
in the end of 1932, could still be strangled (largely
because of the irresolution and muddle-headedness of its
leaders), have grown stronger, not weaker, during the
seven years of Hitler's rule.

I know (from direct acquaintance and active participation) that the Front of these identical forces has
ripened and become more lucid, and that out of it will
proceed the German revolutionary government that will
overthrow Hitler and create the New Germany.

Its task at the Peace Conference will be far from easy,

and one to which there is a solitary parallel in history —
Talleyrand's task at the Congress of Vienna. Talleyrand. having betrayed Napoleon but being a great
French patriot, saved his country at Vienna, where they
believed him when he assured them that Napoleon was
not France nor France Napoleon, though for fourteen
years Napoleon had compromised France even as for
seven years Hitler has compromised Germany.

New Germany hopes that the 'Geneva Congress of
1941' will have as much insight into the actual state of
European affairs as the Vienna Congress had in 1814;
but that Geneva will excel Vienna doubly in courage to
dig down the problem to its very roots; and in a will
directed ahead towards the rebirth and the future of the
West.

### 3. THE AUSTRIAN QUESTION

One of the first and chief matters to be discussed at
the Peace Congress will be the Austrian question.

I know well how complicated it is, too thickly set
with thorns — with a thousand hopes and fears, wishes
and grudges, expressed and unexpressed — for any sort
of simple and easily acceptable solution to be possible.

On the other hand, I must have made so abundantly
clear my invincible persuasion of the inalienable right of
individuals and nations to self-determination, that I am
sure no reader will expect me to believe any valid reasons
could be adduced against the exercise of that right in
this particular case.

New Germany will therefore proclaim the right of
the Austrian people to decide its own future by means

of an absolutely free and uncontrolled popular vote or plebiscite.

As a matter of course this involves the cancellation of the results of Hitler's conquest, i.e. that only men and women who were Austrian citizens before the German invasion will be entitled to vote. In like manner, the popular decision, at a time and in conditions to be prescribed by the Peace Conference, will have to be taken under international supervision and control, and not under the auspices of any government that may be in power there at the time of the plebiscite.

Finally (and this is in my view an essential feature of all such popular decisions) it is better to avoid having a simple alternative, and to have as large as possible a plurality of questions submitted for consideration.

It seems to me that as regards Austria there are three practicable issues:

(1) Joining the Germanic Federation.
(2) Independence of the Red-White-and-Red Schuschnigg Austria.
(3) Re-establishment of the Black-and-Yellow Habsburg-Austria, either as a personal union with Hungary, or as a Danubian Federation consisting of Austria, Hungary, and Czechoslovakia.

I shall venture no prophecy as to what would be the outcome of such a plebiscite, and shall content myself with affirming that in any case New Germany would abide by the plebiscitary decision of its Austrian brethren.

Joining the Germanic Federation must on no account be confounded with the 'Anschluss' to Hitlerian

Germany, or with the 'Anschluss' to the Weimar Republic of which there was talk at one time. As previously explained, New Germany will be federal in structure throughout, will be a league of autonomous provinces, and from its size and population Austria would have a considerable say in the Federation. I have said that it must be a firmly established principle of the federal constitution that all officials in a province must be natives of that province, so that in Austria only Austrians would rule and function, in Bavaria only Bavarians, in Rhineland only Rhinelanders. Thus a strong safeguard of the federal structure would be the direct interest of the local intelligentsia in their own locality.

A Red-White-and-Red Austria would seem thereby to be outclassed in respect of the chief points in its program. Besides, the experiment of St. Germain has shown very clearly the weaknesses of such a scheme — though we must remember that the problem of a larger economic area could be solved within the framework of the European Federation. A decisive matter here, however, will be the question of the time-lag, for the Austrian problem will demand prompt solution, whereas in the most favourable circumstances there is likely to be considerable delay in getting the European Federation into working order.

The re-establishment of Habsburg Austria, whether in the direct form of an Austria-Hungarian double monarchy or in the indirect form of a Danubian Federation, presents itself almost as a matter of course, and would find many supporters among the western powers.

In conformity with my principle that the Austrians

(like any other people) should enjoy the right of self-determination and be left to settle their own affairs, I must point out that the re-establishment of the Habsburg realm is primarily a concern of the Austrian, Hungarian, Czech, and Slovak peoples. Secondly, the demands of Jugoslavia, Rumania, Poland, and Italy for security would run counter to any such re-establishment, and these countries might be expected in this matter to have a more lasting pull at the Peace Conference than would the Austrians, Hungarians, Czechs, and Slovaks in respect of their right to self-determination. Anyone who recalls the terms of the oath which had to be taken by the wearer of the crown of St. Stephen, will feel that there might be some justification for uneasiness on the part of the neighbours of a re-established double monarchy.

In whatever way the Austrian problem might be formulated, and no matter what solution might seem most accordant to the feelings and interests of those concerned, it remains indubitable that the decisive matter must be the right of self-determination of the people of the country, with due regard to its neighbours' sense of the requirements for their safety.

## 4. CZECHOSLOVAKIA AND SUDETENLAND

This basic principle will guide us, not only as regards the settlement of the Austrian question, but also as regards the no less important problem of Czechoslovakia and Sudetenland.

Early in this chapter, on page 81, I declared that an essential preliminary to peace negotiations must be an evacuation by the German troops of all the non-German areas they may have occupied, and a pledge to pay compensation for any damage they may have done. This applies unconditionally to all regions which prior to 1938 formed part of Czechoslovakia.

It would be unwarrantable for New Germany to appeal to the Munich Agreement of September 1938 on the ground that it was 'voluntarily' signed by the Czechoslovak government, for the signature was really extorted by threats and by force, and the agreement brought nearly a million Czechs under foreign (i.e. German) rule.

But no settlement can be sound if it deprives the Sudetenland Germans of their right to self-determination.

Here the application of the principle will need special safeguards if we are to avoid fresh injustices and the risk of further disturbances.

So much intermingled are Germans and Czechs in Sudetenland, that there a vote by districts rather than a general counting of heads will be expedient. Nor must the existence of 'national enclaves' be made a pretext for arbitrary treatment of surrounding majorities of the rival stock. There may have to be local migrations, or some favoured treatment of minorities.—The matter is touched upon in the section on the Jewish problem (p. 73 and foll.).

Since we have expressly recognized, and must unfailingly continue to recognize, that when a people's right to self-determination is being fulfilled, due regard must always be paid to its neighbours' sense of the requirements for their safety, the definitive solution of the

Sudetenland problem will mainly depend upon how far the Czechoslovaks feel that their security will be guaranteed by New Germany. Upon the extent of this sense of security will depend the importance that the future Czechoslovakia will attach to a strategic frontier on the German side of their country.

This will, in its turn, be largely decided by the general solution of the Czechoslovak problem, by the boundaries of the country and its internal construction. Primarily these are matters for the Czechs and Slovaks themselves; secondly, especially as regards the question of boundaries, they are matters for the Peace Congress. As far as New Germany is concerned, that country will certainly consider a large and healthy Czechoslovakia to be a most important pillar of Central European order, and also as a welcome partner in furthering German economic life and in keeping Germany in friendly touch with the Western Slavs.

The Czechs, thanks to the conspicuously European trend of their minds, the admirably democratic organization of their government, and their highly developed science and economic system, seem the predestined instructors of the Ruthenians and Ukrainians, as is manifest from the great achievements of Czechoslovakia in promoting the civilization and the cultural development of Carpathian Ruthenia.

The payment of reparations by New Germany to Czechoslovakia (and Poland) is a matter of obvious justice; the assessment of their amount will be a matter for enquiry and negotiation.

Inasmuch as Czechoslovakia and Poland will both desire prompt settlement of accounts, whereas Germany after Hitler is not likely to have much cash or credit available, the only practicable way of raising funds would seem to be by an international loan, the bulk of which would probably be subscribed in the U.S.A. The most likely way of extracting payments from Germany would be for that country to establish a tobacco monopoly whose profits would be ear-marked for the payment of interest on the loan and the instalments of amortization. Direct control of the business side of the monopoly by representatives of the creditors would provide the necessary guarantees — of course with due regard to political and psychological susceptibilities.

## 5. POLAND, DANZIG, THE CORRIDOR

A bigger affair, and one even more vital to the permanent re-establishment of Europe, will be the management and the solution of the Polish problem. Not only because the present war broke out in relation to Poland, thus showing clearly where 'the shoe pinched', but also because the future peace of Europe turns more upon this matter than upon any other.

Can a mutually satisfactory arrangement be made to reconcile the conflicting interests of the Germans and the Poles? If not, if the 'open sore' between Germanism and Slavism cannot be healed, there can be no lasting peace in Europe. For so long as the sore remained open, how could any Peace Congress make sure that after another twenty-five years the workers and peasants of France, the inhabitants of Canada, South Africa, and Hindostan, might not again take up arms to intervene in a war between Germany and Poland or between Russia and Poland?

The looming of such possibilities, regard for the interests of Europe at large, and (even more) consideration for the joint interests of Germany and Poland, make it possible to discover here also a way out of our difficulties that will be compatible with the rights and the wants of both peoples, and with the provision of guarantees for the safety of the (comparatively weak) Poles.

Immediate evacuation of the parts of Poland occupied by German troops, and a recognition that a war indemnity is due to Poland, will be favourable preliminaries to a settlement, and the offer of German help for the liberation of Eastern Poland may facilitate matters.

The Germans must be prepared to expect that at the Peace Conference demands will probably be voiced for the incorporation of Danzig and even East Prussia into the future Poland.

Apart from the consideration that this would be a fundamental violation of peoples' right to self-determination, such an assignment of territory would inevitably tend to perpetuate a hereditary feud between Germany and Poland.

Seeing that the evacuation of nearly four million Germans from East Prussia would involve widespread misery, and that there would be enormous difficulties — organizational and other — in clearing the regions along the Baltic that have been forcibly colonized by Germans, it is most unlikely that any scheme of this quarrelsome character will be adopted by the Peace Congress. Besides, no conceivable German government could be found to accept it.

More difficult is the question of the Corridor. Here two vital interests are in conflict: the German interest in direct contact with an outlying portion of the Reich; and the Polish interest in a route to the sea.

The recognition that both these interests are vital makes a solution all the more urgent, in order to avert causes of unceasing friction. To begin with, the Germans must admit that for them the only vital matter is the part of the Corridor which ensures direct communication between Pomerania and East Prussia.

Although the region in which the two nations have conflicting vital interests is thus relatively small, this does not make the conflict any easier to evade, for the proposal to have 'a corridor through the corridor' is but a verbal artifice which gives no practical satisfaction.

A solution only becomes possible when we include the Baltic States in the domain of the matters at issue between Germany and Poland, and this will have the advantage of also helping us to solve the extremely difficult Vilna problem.

New Germany will recognize, not only Poland's right to exist, but also that Europe needs a great and powerful Poland.

Poland, the eastern guardian of Europe, the 'limes' of Christendom, must enjoy the material strength and position requisite for the performance of these duties. The cooperation of Poland with the minor Baltic States of Lithuania, Latvia, and Estonia, not only makes it possible for these three European outposts which live under the menace of Russia to be sure of autonomy and of independent development, but also gives Poland her best chance of attaining a broad sea-front on the Baltic.

The juxtaposition of the three petty States to Russian military and naval positions convinces us that their freedom can only be guaranteed by their having the protection of a 'big brother' like Poland; and we may be sure that the Poland of the future will carefully avoid the chief error of the Poland of the past, and will eagerly adopt the federative idea.

Enough! New Germany will feel impelled, both for moral and material reasons, to undo the partition of Poland of which Hitler has been guilty. New Germany will therefore offer Poland her help in regaining Eastern and Southern Poland. We may be sure that no Polish government will renounce Bialystok, Brest-Litovsk, Przemysl, and Lemberg; but we must also consider it unlikely that Moscow will have any inclination for the voluntary surrender of its plunder.

In this matter, too, New Germany will be able to offer the most direct and concrete proof of her determination to make good in the field of reparations. The offer of military aid in regaining Eastern and Southern Poland will do more than the payment of indemnities in hard cash to manifest a complete change in the relations between Germany and Poland, and will react upon the negotiations for Danzig and the northern end of the Corridor. True peace can only be established by respect of the vital interests and the sense of honour of individuals and nations.

### 6. THE BOLSHEVIK PROBLEM

Several times already in this work I have touched on the problem of Russia, which is greatly complicated by the Bolshevik problem.

94

Happily what the latter signifies has of late been made clear and become generally recognized thanks to the close political, military, and economic ties between Nazism and Bolshevism.

Bolshevism is a deadly peril to Europe — a peril which within Europe must be overcome, and on the eastern edge of Europe must be made to keep its distance.

The intra-European conquest will be substantially achieved by the overthrow of Hitler and the partition of Prussia (which is an appendage to Russia).

Keeping Bolshevism at a distance on the east of Europe will be one of the most vital tasks of the Peace Conference, and will necessitate radical measures for safeguarding European peace.

The most urgent matter here is to keep Bolshevism away from the Carpathians, and this can be only successfully achieved by extirpating Bolshevism from Europe.

The fulfilment of that purpose, however vital it may be to Europe at large, does not and must not infringe the vital interests of the Russian people.

Anyone well acquainted with the history of Moscow and Russia will discover there evidence of a process akin to that which has gone on in the history of Prussia and Germany — a part has by force made itself master of the whole, and even made itself master of extensive foreign regions. No one can deny that White Russia and Ukraine, Armenia, Georgia, and the lesser peoples of the Caucasus, were only subjugated by Moscow through the use of force, often after decades of struggle, and that they have never abandoned the longing for freedom. Lenin himself was aware of this, and therefore gave these foreign nationalities at least a formal autonomy — which

95

his Caesarian successor has steadily reduced. I do not feel competent, nor do I regard it as essential to the matter in hand, to discuss whether and how far these subjugated nationalities still aspire to independence and crave for a reunion with Europe. If they do, I am passionately convinced they have a right to be freed, and I should deem it one of the basic duties of a genuinely European Peace Conference to bring to these remote brethren the light of freedom and independence.

Especially as regards White Russia and Ukraine, it would seem that upon the comparatively advanced Western Slavs (the Poles and the Czechs) devolves the fraternal duty of introducing into the European family of nations their so long oppressed and therefore backward Slav brethren the White Russians and the Ukrainians.

This would notably enlarge the buffer regions of Europe on the Bolshevik side; it would supply the highly industrialized nations of Europe with an 'internal colonial' market for their wares; and it would furnish western capital with lucrative opportunities for investment. Besides these obvious advantages, we must likewise remember that the position of Europe in general as a region for agricultural production would be greatly improved; and that there would also be a better chance than there is now for collaboration with Japan, which would find her anti-Bolshevik safeguards thus strengthened.

### 7. IMPORTANCE OF THE WESTERN SLAVS TO EUROPE

I am deliberately stressing, not only the need for compensating Poland and Czechoslovakia by the payment of substantial reparations which may in some measure make good the injustices they have suffered, but also the fact that these peoples and their States are of the utmost importance to the European community.

Two leading motives are at work here.

First of all, by strengthening the position of the Slavs in Eastern Europe we shall give the less numerous peoples of Western Europe the sense that they have a counterpoise on the other side of the Germans in Central Europe.

Secondly, when insisting upon the indisputable right of the Western Slavs to be enrolled on an equal footing, I desire to point out the gains that will ensue for the economics, the politics, and, not least, the culture of Europe.

As regards the former point, Tomorrow's Germany would be so little afraid of being 'encircled' by Latins and Slavs on the west, south, and east, that she would gladly accept the maintenance of old alliances by France, or the formation of new ones, as advantageous to the European Federation (or to the renovated League of Nations), inasmuch as that would make an end once for all of alarms about possible attempts to establish German hegemony. Since the Latin peoples outnumber the Germans and are stronger, since the Anglo-French alliance will assuredly continue after the war, and since the Western Slavs (more especially if the White Russians and the Ukrainians are freed) will rapidly gain importance and influence in Europe — there would be an admirable equipoise between Latins, Germans, and Slavs, so that any racial predominance in Europe would be excluded.

G

As regards what Europe would gain by incorporating the Western Slavs on equal terms, in the long run the cultural advantages would be even greater than the political and economic. This is obvious, and has already been expounded. The most outstanding political gain would be the extinction of Panslavism, a movement no less dangerous to Europe than Pangermanism. For Panslavism gives the Asiatic power of Russia (under the mask of Bolshevism no less than under the mask of Tsarism) an opportunity for interfering in the problems and disputes of Europe. During the last twenty years there have been numerous examples of this.

The cultural gain, finally, cannot be over-estimated. Anyone who has had even a glimpse of the cultural treasures of the Czechs, Poles, Slovaks, Croats, Serbs, and Bulgarians, will be convinced that the older nations of Europe will find in them fountains of youth whose healing waters are essential to the renaissance of the West.

To those who take such an outlook it will seem that the Bolshevik-induced homelessness of the Rumanian, Bulgarian, and Serb Orthodox Churches (like that of the Greek Church, which has also been robbed of its pillars) is an excellent thing for Europe, to which it wholly restores the last of the children that were influenced by Moscow — Byzantium.

# CHAPTER FOUR

# EUROPEAN FEDERATION

## I. A EUROPEAN CIVIL WAR

THE historical demonstration that in the war which began at the close of August 1939 the trigger was pulled by the Hitler System's will-to-power (behind which stood the traditional Prussian imperialism), and by the Bolshevik will-to-power (mainly inspired by the Pan-slavist tendencies of Tsarism), must be supplemented by an account of the ideological character of the war, which gives it the aspect of a European Civil War.

For the fact is that in every country, throughout Europe, there is a party opposed to the official policy of its own land: in Germany no less than in France; in Finland no less than in Portugal; in Ireland as well as in Rumania. No matter whether this internal opposition is large or small, whether it is evoked and sustained more by Hitlerian propaganda or by Bolshevik ideology, no one can deny that the war is substantially ideological, is a 'war of religions' in which the adversaries are not nations but groups of zealots. This is typical of civil war.

American observers, with the advantage of distance, have plainly discerned this characteristic of the war, comparing it with the American War of Secession, in which political and economic differences were doubtless at work, but which was essentially an ideological war, and for this reason procreated the U.S.A. in its present form.

The recognition that the war is really a civil war, that it is ideological or almost religious in type, finds expression in the hopes of the peoples and the avowed aims of the belligerents.

Hitherto in this book I have been expounding the hopes and aims of the German people as follows:

Liberation from the dominion of the junkers, the generals, and the great capitalists by the establishment of a socialist and economic order.

Liberation from the dominion of Prussia by a league of the German tribes within the framework of a free Germanic Federation.

As regards the hopes and aims of the whole 'European Party' in this 'Civil War', there remains a third to mention:

The transformation of Europe into a league of free nations.

For centuries the poets and imaginative writers of all the peoples of Europe have been dreaming of this unity, the best thinkers have contributed to the idea, and during the terrible years from 1920 to 1940 the economists have again and again been forced to admit that their plans will remain fruitless so long as 'Europe' does not really exist.

Notable persons, among whom Aristide Briand and Count Coudenhove-Kalergi should be especially mentioned, have made admirable efforts in this direction, achieving important preliminary advances, but the peoples still lag far behind these bold pioneers.

Only of late, in the theoretical disputes that preceded the Civil War, and in the ideological clarifications which it has promoted among all the peoples, have widespread aspirations for unity arisen, a knowledge of its importance, a longing for collaboration, and a will to bring it about. The Pangermans' recent and present attempts to achieve the conquest of Europe, with the consequent revival of memories of the earlier attempts of Napoleon and Charles V, have made it clear that no one nation in Europe is strong enough to subjugate all the others and establish a United European Empire modelled on the Roman Empire of old.

The torrents of blood in which the originators of such schemes have been or will be drowned will not have been poured forth in vain, should the peoples of Europe learn thereby that they are all members one of another, not as servants of one nation or one man, but with equal standing as members of one family, as voluntary constituents of a European Federation.

Maybe, so far, in my disquisitions on the need for European unity, I have not sufficiently emphasized the federal idea, which was uncongenial to the centralist trend of the nineteenth century. Noteworthy in itself is the fact that we now speak of a European Federation, and have dropped the term 'Paneuropa'. The federal scheme is equally essential to the successful solution of numerous political, economic, and cultural problems both within the various States of Europe and within Europe itself.

When, therefore, I now proceed to discuss certain practical tasks that will devolve upon the European Federation, they are all to be considered on the provisos of interconnexion, equality of rights, and voluntariness which must be the pillars of every federation.

## 2. GUARANTEES OF SECURITY AND DISARMAMENT

Before I begin a sketch of that European Federation, a picture of which must loom in the minds of all the soldiers (whether they are aware of it or not) as the aim of the sacrifices they are making, let me turn back to the practical political question of the guarantees for security upon whose provision will depend fruitful negotiations for the establishment of a new order in Europe.

Between us and this new order stands the war, the extent of whose sacrifices is still uncertain, but whose most immediate aim cannot but be the 'never again' of the attacked nations, which will only enjoy tranquillity when guarantees of material security have been furnished, and only then be ready to discuss far-reaching plans.

For the very reason that New Germany appreciates this psychological attitude and admits it to be justified, and for the very reason that New Germany is assured of the need for permanent collaboration and ardently desires it, New Germany will be perfectly willing to provide the requisite guarantees.

In my account of the prerequisites for an armistice, of the federalization of Germany, of the democratic and socialist reconstruction of Germany within, and of the radical destruction of Prussian militarism which of old has guided Germany's attitude towards her neighbours, I have already expounded the most important of the guarantees that will be given by New Germany.

Even more conspicuous, however, and therefore able to have a greater effect abroad, will be Germany's decisive adoption of the principle of equal rights directly peace is signed.

New Germany will agree to the destruction of the Siegfried Line under the supervision of British and French experts while agreeing to the maintenance of the Maginot Line!

New Germany will likewise agree to France's maintaining her present alliances, both during and after the establishment of the European Federation, whereas Germany will promptly denounce her alliance with Italy and Japan. Finally New Germany would be prepared to renounce the ownership of Heligoland, and this would involve a marked increase in the security of the western powers as against Germany.

The status of the Belt and the Sound will urgently need consideration under the same department. Hitler's successful subjugation of Denmark in April 1940 without striking a blow has shown how impracticable it is that the keys of the Baltic should remain 'in the hands of a child'. Whether this question can best be settled by the incorporation of Denmark into the British Empire, or by the establishment of British fortresses in the 'Gibraltar of the Baltic' will be matters for enquiry and negotiation. In one or other of these ways, guarantees would be provided against future attacks by Germany (or Russia), and enhanced protection would be secured by Poland.

But the most decisive guarantee of general security, and the only one which could content all the European peoples, would be a general agreement to disarm.

Apart from the political question of security, we are here concerned with the economic and financial argument that unless there is a notable restriction of armaments bankruptcy or impoverishment will be general among the States of Europe. We have merely to imagine what will be the condition of national finance everywhere when the war draws to a close, and we shall see that collapse and pauperization can only be avoided by reducing to a very modest fraction the milliards that have of late been squandered on armaments.

But such a comprehensive reduction will only be possible if there is a general agreement to disarm jointly and simultaneously, the process being subjected to reciprocal control.

The carrying out and the control of disarmament will be the concern of a sub-committee of the Peace Conference. Enough here to say from the German side that within the general staff a number of officers must mutually exercise the control, for experience has shown that effective control must be from within.

The climax of this reciprocal disarmament on the part of the nations of Europe would be the creation of a composite European army.

Its national constituents could be so constituted as to give the European peoples a hundred-per-cent guarantee of security as against one another. Britain, for instance, might supply the aviation contingent; France, the heavy guns and the tanks; Germany, the light artillery and the infantry; Poland, the cavalry; Czechoslovakia, the pioneers. The neutral States, especially Spain and Italy, would for the time being only undertake a systematic reduction of their national armies. The formation of this European army would be an additional and extremely important factor of security, and the defensive capacity of Europe as a whole would not be in the least impaired.

## 3. POLITICAL COLLABORATION

Our earnest desire for a European Federation and our determination to establish it must not blind us to the immense difficulties that will have to be overcome. In my view the chief reason why so little support has been given to any of the plans hitherto mooted has been that they were all designed from a ready-made picture and paid too little heed to extant national institutions — moss-grown with antiquity and deeply rooted.

In contrast to these plans, of which new variants are published almost every day, I myself (true to my conservative principles) start from the conviction that all historical processes need a considerable time to ripen. I am also guided by the general experience that amalgamations had better begin with the minimum, for then we can be sure that as time passes the attachments will become firmer and more numerous.

To every advocate of the notion of a European Federation — which in 1940 must surely include all thoughtful Europeans — can be earnestly commended a study of the British Commonwealth. There we have: a minimum of coercion, a maximum of freedom; due regard for diverging local interests and respect for national susceptibilities; the maintenance of time-honoured institutions, even though they are often inconvenient; the avoidance of undue levelling, and instead a deliberate preservation of national or local manners and customs.

In a word, the amalgamation is to be made effective without thereby sensibly or visibly altering the previous methods, rules, or ways. Here is the best recipe for the establishment of a European Federation.

To demand at the outset the establishment of a federal government, a federal executive, and the like, would only raise needless difficulties, perhaps amounting to impossibilities. (Once more I say, look at the British Empire.)

At the start, of course, the European Federation can only be a voluntary union of European States, access to which will be open to every European State that complies with the prescribed regulations. It will be advantageous to the Federation to make membership a thing to be coveted by every European State.

Among the conditions of membership will be that the candidate State must be subject to the reign of law, both in home affairs and in foreign relations; it must recognize the arbitral powers of the Federation; must participate in the Permanent Court of International Justice at The Hague and in the (renovated) League of Nations, and in any international institutions established by these.

The most important feature of the Federation, and at the same time the chief advantage of membership, will be the collective security of the members, as maintained by their reciprocal guarantees and by their mutual pledges to combine in order to resist an attack made from without upon any member of the Federation.

The enormous advantages, alike political, military, and financial, of having a joint armed force are so obvious that the members of the European Federation will establish one sooner or later, even though to begin with it may take a more traditional form than the one sketched above, having specifically distinct national contingents.

The relations of the European Federation to the League of Nations will be mainly determined by the reconstruction of the latter in the sense of a worldwide representation of continental groups.

## 4. ECONOMIC COLLABORATION

Much closer (and therefore doubly attractive to outsiders) can be economic collaboration. It is likely to be developed forthwith — and experience teaches that joint economic advantages form the strongest cement for social cohesion.

The gradual abolition of all customs barriers upon free trade; the discontinuance of insistence upon passports and other hindrances to freedom of movement; the systematic cultivation of international economic and financial relations; unified currency systems; the joint performance of mighty schemes — such will be the chief methods of economic collaboration among the States that will be members of the European Federation, and the resulting advantages will be so overwhelming that any sceptical or hesitant outsiders will soon be eager to join.

Collaboration of the national economies within the European Federation will help to guard the members against 'trade crises', an effect that will be strengthened by the unity of labour laws and labour-protection schemes throughout the Federation.

Important contributions thereto will be made by the increasingly unified action of the economic aggregate of the European Federation in world-politics and upon the world-market.

Additional possibilities for economic collaboration will be provided by the facilitation of freedom of traffic and trade, the open chances the citizens will have for settling in one another's countries, the assimilation of their respective systems of weights and measures and of coinage, unified customs tariffs as against non-members, a common policy as concerns stocks and shares, and what not.

Of course it is likely enough that there will be varying grades of collaboration among the members, such as have been begun of late between England and France. Here, too, the principle of the utmost flexibility is more important than the principle of the utmost unity.

## 5. CULTURAL COLLABORATION

The most obvious of all the features of the Federation will be, and should be, the cultural collaboration of its members.

Among the peoples of Europe, which have too long been spellbound by narrow national ideas, it is time to revive an awareness of their historical and cultural assocation.

Nothing will contribute more to this awakening than a knowledge of the national peculiarities of the various peoples of Europe, for that will make them respect one another, and take pride in the multifariousness of the West, inasmuch as variety is not only the charm of Europe but its very essence.

A noble rivalry of national spirits and national arts,

an 'Olympiad of the mind', should be inaugurated to bring together the peoples of the European Federation through regular publications and other suitable arrangements, as a supplement of the physical Olympiad revived at Athens in 1900, and rightly regarded as one of the finest examples of international collaboration.

Appropriate to the cultural collaboration of the members of the European Federation would be that they should manifest their interdependency in their educational systems, and tolerate nothing that might run counter to it. A good thing would be to have a special committee appointed to attend to such matters, and exercise a censorship over schoolbooks. In science, also, there should be close collaboration; and the arts of various countries should fertilize one another, as they could effectively do through the instrumentality of a European Academy.

The increasing importance that is being attached to the work of the Churches would also help to promote awareness of cultural collaboration, for the spirit of Christianity is the most fundamental bond of the unity of the West.

# CHAPTER FIVE

# THE COLONIAL PROBLEM

EVEN within this sketchy account of the Problems of the Peace Conference and of the European Federation it is desirable to consecrate a section to the colonial problem, for the Conference will certainly have to consider the German claim to colonies. Furthermore the treatment of the colonial problem will give a crucial example of the new spirit that will be essential to the establishment of a new order in Germany and in Europe.

Speaking generally, the colonial problem must not be solved, either for Germany or for the other European States which have or desire colonies, in such a way that the limited (and for various reasons dwindling) colonial areas can ever again change masters in consequence of an intra-European war.

There must be an entirely new attitude towards this problem, and that will entail a new solution.

The first essential is to recognize that nowadays the colonial problem is mainly a problem of raw materials. Subordinate to this are such questions as that of economics, settlement, fields for investment, etc. Last of all come questions of prestige and national security.

Such a view of the colonial problem will steadily gain ground with the establishment of a new political and economic order in Europe, and the consequent growing solidarity of the European peoples.

New Germany, for instance, will not claim that she

has more right to colonies than other States, such as Poland or Czechoslovakia. The arguments that Germany might advance on behalf of being put in possession of colonies might be advanced with equal force by other European countries that have no colonies.

Inasmuch as a perennial struggle for colonies (whose size and lucrativeness cannot be indefinitely magnified) must be rendered impossible, a new sort of solution must be found, and this is that certain regions of Africa shall be jointly administered by the European States which hitherto have had no colonies.

To avert the suspicion that such a formulation may be a cloak for a predatory campaign on the part of the 'have-nots' against the 'haves', and also to facilitate the acceptance of the scheme, it must be clearly understood at the outset that England, France, Italy, and Spain — the chief colonial powers of Europe — will deliberately stand aside as possible beneficiaries. (The same consideration applies to the non-African colonies of the other European powers.)

Thus the scheme would apply to the former German colonies in Africa and to the African possessions of Belgium and Portugal. These large, valuable, and still for the most part undeveloped, areas would be placed under the joint administration of all the European powers, with the exception of the four great colonial powers previously named.

With this end in view, the European States other than those purposely excluded would jointly from a 'European Colonial Company' (E.C.C.) to which each State would subscribe funds proportional to the number of its inhabitants. Investments, administrative posts, and possibilities of settlement would be allotted pro rata to the various States that had formed the E.C.C., subject to adjustment every decade in accordance with the census returns of the nations concerned. Any national quota not taken up would be open to the public on loan, but here also subject to decennial revision and recall.

The European Colonial Company would pledge itself to respect the rights of the previous owners or mandataries of the regions it would take over.

To the previous owners or mandataries must, above all, be assigned a ninety-nine year right to the returns on the basis of the average yield of the last ten years. Furthermore the E.C.C. would guarantee the maintenance of existing material and personal rights, especially the tenure of their posts by extant officials, military officers, and subordinate soldiers — for life or while fit for service, previous rights to pensions, etc., being scrupulously preserved. The appointment of new officials would only be made as needed, once more pro rata. Military officers and subordinate soldiers would be appointed as vacancies arose, but there would be no increase in the staffs as they existed on December 31, 1938.

The E.C.C. would also guarantee that the flags that had flown over the respective territories should continue to fly there, but would have the right of hoisting its own flag beside the other; it would continue to use whatever had been the official language in any locality, but with the right to use a second official language as well, should this be expedient anywhere for administrative purposes. Thus all the administrations would be placed on an equal footing.

Future officials and settlers would attend, to begin with, a course of study in colonial schools to be set up in the respective countries of Europe, and the teaching in these would be unified as far as possible.

The E.C.C. would lay especial stress upon the advancement of the indigenes of the colonies, regarding itself as their guardian; and when the natives developed they would, as far as possible, be associated in the work of administration.

The E.C.C. would endeavour to make with the great colonial powers agreements that would be to their mutual advantage. The great colonial powers would also be entitled to join with the E.C.C. in the furtherance of all or some of the latter's possessions.

New Germany would be prepared to assign unconditionally to the E.C.C. all its own colonial rights, even its most recent ones, for it would regard the formation of this body as a just and generally satisfactory solution.

It seems important to point out that the joint cultivation of interests within the E.C.C. would have favourable repercussions upon the political collaboration of the various States; and that the great civilizing work that would be associated with the effective opening-up of Africa would give a powerful impetus to economics and science — and be most beneficial to the youths of Europe. Having great duties to perform makes people young, vigorous, and cheerful. That is what Europe needs.

# CHAPTER SIX

# WAR AIMS

SUMMARIZING the ideas hitherto expounded, we can make the following list of war aims:

(1) Overthrow of Hitler and Hitlerism.

(2) Annihilation of Prussian power politics by the federalization of Germany.

(3) Restoration of liberty to the Czechoslovaks and the Poles.

(4) Reparations to be paid by Germany to the Poles and the Czechoslovaks.

(5) Right of self-determination for the inhabitants of Austria, Sudetenland, and the Danzig region.

(6) The safeguarding of France by the destruction of the Siegfried line while the Maginot line remains intact.

(7) Joint defence against the Bolshevik peril.

(8) General disarmament under reciprocal control.

(9) Expansion of the Anglo-French economic alliance into an economic collaboration of Europe at large.

(10) The establishment of a European Federation within the framework of a renovated League of Nations.

The foregoing 'Peace Aims of New Germany' are primarily dedicated to the German people, which less than any other is in a position to grasp the nature and meaning of this war, or to understand its outbreak and its course. Seven years of propaganda have clouded the minds of Germans within the Reich; seven years of the

Hitlerian Reign of Terror have in part intimidated them and in part coarsened them. Nevertheless I am sure that the feelings and thoughts of the German people will endorse these Peace Aims; and that the German people wants to take part in the upbuilding of a New Europe which it longs for no less ardently than do the peoples of other lands.

The latter should be convinced by these proposals that Tomorrow's Germany will be ready to give the requisite moral and material guarantees to show the eagerness of the German people to be incorporated in New Europe.

I know that the dead of the war of 1914-1918 and the dead of the war of 1940-      bequeath as their supreme legacy:

the upbuilding of a New Europe.

# CHAPTER ONE

# PHILOSOPHICAL FOUNDATIONS

## I. INTRODUCTORY

IN contradistinction to the hitherto prevailing liberal and mechanistic views, we start with the belief that a people or a nation is an organism, a living body, with definite peculiarities of a corporeal, mental, and spiritual kind.

From this it follows that to the history of a nation there applies the eternal law of organic life, the 'die and become', a biological compulsion to pass along the inevitable road from the cradle to the grave, from the apple-seed by way of the fruit-bearing tree to the dead wood. This application of biological laws to the course of national life does not invalidate the metaphysical premises of fate and of the activity of God — any more than our knowledge and recognition of the inevitable movement of the individual's life from birth to death can either 'explain' or invalidate the enigma of his having become a human being or the form taken by his nature.

## 2. RACE—PEOPLE—NATION

If, therefore, we try to explain the origin of a people, we must never forget that we can do so only within the limits to which all human knowledge is subject. That is to say we can only explain it within that causal world outside or above which we recognize the governance of the fate that primarily sets causality to work and determines its trend.

From this outlook we perceive that a people is an amalgam of various races, even as a child mingles within itself in definite proportions both maternal and paternal 'racial' constituents.

To the biological influences of this racial amalgam are superadded the geopolitical influences of situation, climate, diet, etc.; and, finally, the historical effects of the dispute one nation may have had with another, of internal adjustments, of personal ripening, and what not.

Out of these threefold constituents of race, country, and history, the 'people' is formed — though we must again emphasize the limits imposed upon this causal explanation by referring to the becoming, the genesis, of a human being, whose essential character and form are outside the domain of causality.

Applying these considerations to Europe (to which Russia does not belong, never has belonged, and never will belong), this signifies that the peoples of Europe have originated out of the same racial constituents (Dr. Günther, the famous ethnologist, distinguishes from four to five primary races in Europe), which in different countries are mingled in various proportions. In this fundamentally similar racial composition we discern the explanation of the typically European or western civilization as that of one family of peoples in which the individual children (read, 'individual peoples') represent various minglings of the parents (read, 'races').

To the effects of this varying racial admixture within the different members of the European or western family of peoples were superadded the effects of differences in the countries they inhabited, thanks to which their visages were further differentiated; and, finally, the effects of their respective histories, which even more strongly influenced the further formation of the various peoples. As a result has been produced the extraordinary diversity of the western peoples, which nevertheless all have, owing to their racial kinship, one and the same rhythm of western culture, and have all been subjected to the same vital laws of this family of peoples.

The concepts 'race' and 'people' (including family of peoples, or cultural circle) having been thus explained, the 'nation' obviously discloses itself to be a 'people' that has become more fully self-conscious. A people whose history has taught it its own specific peculiarity becomes a nation, which simultaneously presents itself as the ripe stage, the fully adult stage, of the people which is 'at home' in a specific area. (Compare this with the 'awareness of personality' that ensues in the individual as a result of his experiences and adventures.)

At this stage of our exposition it will become plain why Young Germany insists that in the new epoch inaugurated by the war of 1914-1918 the German people is undergoing its development into nationhood as the last people of the western cultural circle; and why Young Germany finds therein the reason for the repercussion of the German Revolution upon the whole western cultural circle.

## 3 . RHYTHM OF HISTORY

From the foregoing dissertations it will have become plain that we accept the validity of Oswald Spengler's brilliantly formulated law of the rise and fall of the cultural circle—in this instance the western cultural circle; and that we perceive therein a great law of motion of all organic life, the law of birth, maturity, and death.

As something essentially new, we supplement this law of motion which is comparable to the movement of the earth round the sun, by a second law of motion — one whose manifestations I myself described several years ago, giving it the name of the Law of Triune Polarity. Its working may be compared to the rotation of the earth on its own axis.

Empirical study of the course of development within the western cultural circle shows certain regularities, which on closer examination may be systematized as follows. We discern epochs of constraint or fixity alternating with epochs of unconstraint or revolution. A study of dates shows that such an epoch lasts from 140 to 150 years, and is followed by another epoch which lasts about the same time. Without transcending the limits of this introductory work, I may point out that the last three phases of transition were: 1789-1799, the great French Revolution; 1640-1649, the English Revolution under Cromwell; about 1500 began the mighty revolution we call the Reformation (America having been discovered a few years before). Going farther back in European history we come to such caesuras as 1350 (Hansa, Golden Bull, etc.); towards 1200, etc. Herbert Blank's book, *Schleicher? Hitler? — Cromwell?*, published by the Verlag Lindner (Leipzig, 1932), contains a detailed account of this 'Rhythm of History'.

If we study more closely the ideas and the forms of these various epochs, we discover the remarkable fact that we only have to do with two conflicting ideas, two opposing poles, between which the pendulum of history swings unceasingly: the idea of constraint, and the idea of unconstraint; or, we may say, conservatism and liberalism.

Should we try to transfer into organic life these two ideas and the change from one to the other, we shall easily recognize the two main forces of organic life, the self-preservative impulse and the species-preservative impulse. The first makes the self, the ego, the second makes the species, the community of like persons, the we, into the centre of the universe. The first is the soil out of which the ego-idea, the second is the soil out of which the we-idea grows.

It is needless to explain why we identify the ego-idea with liberalism, and the we-idea with conservatism, since after what has been said it is obvious that we reject the attempt to grade their respective values, for we regard this as non-organic. Just as you cannot say that day is more valuable than night, or night than day, since each determines the other, and both are merely the poles between which the pendulum of the earth's rotation swings; so you cannot say that the ego-idea is worth more than the we-idea, or the we-idea worth more than the ego-idea, that liberalism is preferable to conservatism, or conservatism to liberalism, since each determines the other, and they are but the poles between which life swings on its course from birth to death. A simple comparison may make this twofold law-abidingness easier to understand. Within the law from apple-seed to apple-tree to dead wood, fulfils itself annually the rhythm of summer and winter — a rhythm whose forms of expression are chiefly determined by the law of age.

We prove, therefore, that the 'ideas' of conservatism

and liberalism continually replace one another on the visage of a cultural circle, determining the thoughts and feelings of human beings, and thereby determining the forms of their life.

In accordance with the three-dimensional character of all organic life in body, mind, and soul (the bodily plane representing the relation of human beings to things; the mental plane, the relation of human beings to one another; and the soul plane, the relation of man to God), each of these ideas manifests itself equably and simultaneously upon these three planes of life. In an epoch when the 'we-idea' is dominant, we therefore observe constraint, conservatism, an economy in which the we-idea prevails, a social order characterized by the we-idea, a cultivation of the we-idea; and conversely when the ego-idea is dominant we notice an economy in which the ego-idea prevails, a society of the ego-idea, a cultivation of the ego-idea.

In current parlance (regarding the now declining ego-idea as characteristic of liberalism) we therefore speak of 'capitalism' when liberalism is dominant on the bodily economic plane; speak of 'individualism' when liberalism is dominant on the mental-social plane (i.e. in the State); speak of 'materialism' when liberalism is dominant culturally and on the plane of the soul (i.e. in religious matters).

This triad of capitalism, individualism, and materialism is what we discern as the forms of liberalism that exist in the receding stage of the western cultural circle.

As contrasted with this triad of liberalism, the we-idea of conservatism likewise manifests itself equably on the three planes of life: as 'socialism' on the bodily economic plane; as 'nationalism' on the mental-social plane (the State); and as 'popular idealism' on the soul-cultural plane (religion).

This triad of socialism, nationalism, and popular idealism is what we discern as the forms of conservatism that exist in the advancing stage of the western cultural circle.

When we have mastered this basic outlook, we find it easy to perceive the character of the French Revolution, as a victory of liberalism, and that of the English Revolution as a victory of conservatism; for we know that at about 1500 the liberal idea was becoming dominant, and that at about 1350 a conservative epoch was beginning — and the differing vocabularies used in those old days, or the varying forms dependent upon the different phases of ripeness, will no longer be able to hide the underlying ideas.

The law of triune polarity not only gives us an entirely new explanation and appraisement of the past, but also gives us an appraisement of the present and an interpretation of the future. We perceive that the times are being fulfilled, for the dominant epoch of liberalism and its forms (capitalism, individualism, and materialism) is drawing to a close, and ever since August 1914 the pendulum of the clock of fate has been swinging towards a new epoch when conservatism will be dominant in the forms of socialism, nationalism, and popular idealism, whose mighty uprise and eruption we call the German Revolution.

I should like to make it plain that acceptance of these philosophical foundations is not to be regarded as an essential preliminary to the approval of the political and economic disquisitions that follow. But I regarded it and regard it as incumbent on me, as a matter of personal decency, to allude, however briefly, to the deeper wells from which I myself have drawn the constructive forms I am going to expound, although others may wish to study these forms for purely opportunist reasons, or may arrive at the same results in very different ways.

Anyhow I should like to insist that it is of the utmost importance for everyone who wishes to play an active part to have a sound and unified philosophical standpoint (which for others may seem a mere hypothesis) — all the more because the multifariousness of life will continually present new tasks 'outside the blue-prints'; and because the performance of these will (consciously or unconsciously) be facilitated by waters drawn from the deep wells of philosophy.

## 4. MARXISM

It also seemed indispensable to begin Part Three by a clear statement of the philosophical foundations of German socialism, that we might thus early explain the internal and fundamental opposition of German socialism to international Marxism — a matter to which allusion will frequently have to be made in the sequel. For us National Socialists, of course, there is no question of Marxism being an invention of 'the Jew Marx' specially designed to lead the German workers into error or even into poverty. But for us Marxism is a socialism both liberal and alien, a doctrine whose liberal factors necessarily unfit it for the upbuilding of the socialist (i.e. conservative) future, and one whose program cannot but involve it in the decline of liberalism. This applies quite as much to the constitutional Marxism of the S.P.D. (Socialist Party of Germany) as to the 'revolutionary' Marxism of the K.P.D. (Communist Party of Germany), as is shown convincingly enough by the fact that the S.P.D. is no less hostile to National Socialism than is the K.P.D.

There was nothing primarily 'wrongheaded' about this liberal alienism. It was simply due to the fact that the longing for socialism began to find expression at a time when the ego-idea, liberalism that is to say, was in the ascendant. In these circumstances the socialist struggle of the workers had either to face inevitable defeat (as the Peasants War of 1525 faced defeat because then, likewise, liberalism was in favour), or else to adapt itself to the dominant liberal ideas.

Thanks to Marx, Engels, Kautsky, etc. (all typical liberals both by origin and by nature), socialism took the liberal path towards alienism, as was plainly shown by its relation to the International, its class-war tactics, and its materialist philosophy.

For that reason, and only for that reason, it will be impossible for Marxism to play a formative role in the coming development, and for that reason Marxism will be involved in the decline of liberalism.

The author has intentionally left the above paragraphs exactly as they were written in 1931 in order to show how the truth of what he then wrote has been confirmed by subsequent facts. The catastrophe of the Marxian parties in Italy, Germany, and Austria — in part also in Spain — is only comprehensible when we realize that it was the fateful consequence of the dying-out of the liberal idea and of its associated forms. For neither the differences in strategy as worked out by Marxism in its two main trends of communism and social democracy, nor yet the differences in tactics as practised by Marxism during its death struggles in Germany and Austria, did anything to save it from its fate.

Moreover, if we contemplate the position of the Marxian parties in the other countries of Europe we see that neither in its revolutionary nor in its reformist form does Marxism play any decisive part in European events. (In this connexion it is interesting to note that such part as Marxian parties still play is directly proportional to their attachment to the nation, and that in accordance therewith the numerous and welcome attempts at the renovation of Marxism necessarily start with a renewed enquiry into the relation between the nation and the workers.)[1]

Nevertheless, in view of the fact that 'Fight Marxism' has become a modern catchword, it seems to me only just and decent to point out how much the Marxian labour movement has achieved on behalf of the broad masses of the people, and especially to stress the importance of the trade unions.

But a knowledge and an admission of these things makes it all the more necessary to enquire why Marxism has been a political failure, and here I am not so much concerned with hair-splittings about Marxian theory as with the political practice of the Marxian parties. It is this which must above all be kept in the limelight during the investigations which follow.

[1] C.f. the book *Volk und Arbeiter* by Wenzel Jaksch, a German social democrat of Sudetenland.

# CHAPTER TWO

# GERMAN SOCIALISM

## 1. THE CRISIS OF CAPITALISM

IN the forefront of every consideration of economics stands the question of its function. The man of the people always answers as follows: 'The function of a nation's economic system is to satisfy all the citizens' needs for food, clothing, and shelter, and to put by reserves for troublous times.'

Minor details apart, an economic system which does these things secures the general approval of those whose bodily needs are thus satisfied.

These considerations explain, not only the existence and the duration of the liberal (i.e. the capitalist) economic system, but also its present crisis and its approaching end. Independently of all anti-capitalist theories, the capitalist economy would persist (in Germany) if it could continue to perform its task of ensuring for all Germans a sufficiency of food, clothing, and shelter. The 'crisis of capitalism', therefore, is not an outcome of the socialist movement, but, on the contrary, its main cause.

For it is an obvious fact that the capitalist economic system can no longer perform its function (as above defined), this being plainly shown by the huge numbers of the unemployed, the proletarianization of the middle class, the ruin of the peasantry, and the failure to provide openings for the members of the rising generation.

When within the domain of causality we seek explana-
tions of the breakdown of capitalism, we find that the
three most essential factors of the capitalist economy all
contribute to it equally:

*a.* The capitalist economic policy of a centralized worldwide system of production, exchange, and the gold standard.

*b.* The capitalist economic law which decrees that
'private property is sacred'.

*c.* The capitalist economic form of industrialization,
mechanization, rationalization, and gigantic enterprises.

It is necessary to indicate briefly the disastrous consequences of these three features of the capitalist economic
system, as prelude to a demonstration of the opposing
trends which must be taken by German socialism.

Our view that capitalism is the economic system of
liberalism is fundamentally distinct from the Marxian
and the Hitlerian (or fascist) views.

To both the latter is attached an appraisement, which
becomes intensified to invectives against the supporters of
capitalism.

Marxism, with its unhistorical way of looking at things,
is further inclined to describe all earlier economic
systems as capitalist, or at least quasi-capitalist, with
which socialism is contrasted as something entirely new.

Thus the Marxians fail to recognize that capitalism is
ideologically linked with liberalism, prior to the dominion
of which there was an entirely different economic system
ideologically akin to socialism, though of course differing
from socialism in form.[1]

In like manner the Hitlerians (and the fascists) fail to

[1] *Abendlandische Revolution* [The Revolution in the West], a recent book by
the Prague social democrat Emil Franzel, is a notable exception to the common-
place Marxian sociology

understand that the ties between capitalism and liberalism are inseparable, and they look forward to destroying
liberalism while keeping the capitalist system intact.

On the other hand the National Socialists, while
recognizing the importance of capitalism because of its
great achievements, are convinced that by internal
causes the system is doomed.

### A. Capitalist Economic Policy

Capitalist economic policy is based upon the open
world-market, worldwide free trade, and the international
gold standard. But all three of these principles were irre-
parably destroyed by the war [of 1914-1918], and from our
'organic' outlook the war was only the expression of a
revolution, not the cause of this revolution. For:

*a.* During the war the uncivilized and semi-civilized
countries (India, China, South America, North Africa,
South Africa) started gigantic industries of their own;
and when, after the war, the two countries where manufacturing enterprise had been longest established, Britain
and Germany — backed up by the U.S.A., which during
the war had been transformed from an importing country
into an exporting country — tried to supply their old
markets, they were faced everywhere by locally-produced
manufactured articles. These locally-manufactured goods
could be sold much cheaper, because wages were lower,
and nothing had to be added to the prices on account of
freight and customs dues.

*b.* In connexion with the war, vigorous nationalist
movements began everywhere, especially among the
semi-colonial and wholly colonial peoples. Their nationalist struggles for liberty were always linked with

attempts to boycott 'white goods', attempts of which Gandhi's spinning-wheel is one typical instance, and another is the universal movement in China against imported commodities (a movement which went on regardless of the disturbances resulting from the wars between the generals). The economic policy of independent Turkey took a similar line to those of Persia and Egypt. Everywhere the struggle for national freedom continued side by side with a campaign against 'white goods', i.e. against the capitalism of Europe and the U.S.A.

*c.* Another change having important consequences was — in connexion with the Bolshevik Revolution — the disappearance of Russia as a consumer of the goods produced by the older manufacturing countries. More than a hundred and sixty million customers disappeared from the 'world-market', to say nothing of the developing possibilities of Russia as an exporter.

The world-market, and trade generally, were completely upset by the cooperation of these and other factors. Then came the break-away of more and more countries from the international gold standard, causing shocks to which the German reparations contributed jolts of their own.

Since all these causes remain in operation, and from their nature are likely to act with increasing strength, there is no prospect that the foundations of capitalist economic policy will ever again be firmly established.

Although the capitalist world clung convulsively to the hope that this was nothing more than a transient crisis, that hope has been cruelly frustrated by the course of world trade.

According to statistics published by the Geneva Bureau of the League of Nations, the trade of the world as reckoned in milliards of French francs has been:

| Year | Imports | Exports |
|------|---------|---------|
| 1929 | 813 | 735 |
| 1930 | 662 | 586 |
| 1931 | 505 | 415 |
| 1932 | 319 | 285 |
| 1933 | 289 | 266 |
| 1934 | 273 | 252 |

The mighty and successful efforts of Russia and Japan leave the manufacturing States of Europe (where production is more costly) no chance of ever regaining their old position as exporters; and it has to be remembered that the U.S. policy of economic isolation, in conjunction with the Empire policy inaugurated by Britain at Ottawa, tends to make matters worse. To the European States the 'crisis' therefore presents itself as a structural one, which can only be overcome by an entire transformation of the economic system.

### B. Capitalist Economic Law

The capitalist economic law which decrees that 'private property is sacred', that 'a man can do what he likes with his own', was also completely undermined by the war [of 1914-1918]. In the hearts of the people there spread a feeling that there was something fundamentally unjust about a system which repudiated the moral demand for safeguards against pauperization and lack of bread, which brought about or maintained an anti-social cleavage of the population into strata of exploiters and exploited, and excluded the great majority of the citizens from any share in the property, guidance, and advance of the nation. To every individual it became plain that such an unrestricted right on the part of an owner 'to do what he liked with his own' conflicted with the vital interests of the people, and that there could be no inner justification for such a right at a time when the whole nation was being called upon to shed its blood in the defence of 'property'.

These experiences have made it impossible that the capitalist law concerning the 'sacredness of private property' should ever again secure recognition from the German people.

Of decisive significance in this matter is the distinction between the goods which can be augmented in quantity as much as you please, and those which cannot be so augmented because they are monopolies.

Since the very existence of a people depends upon certain goods of which there is only a restricted quantity (land, the raw materials that lie beneath the surface of the land, and — with certain reservations — the means of production in general), people as a whole are directly dependent upon those who own such monopolies. If the (capitalist) right of private property is considered to be valid as regards these monopolies, then persons to whom the monopolies 'belong' can dispose at will of the life and death of millions of their fellow-countrymen. The economic power which thus accrues to the owners of monopolies is the essential curse of capitalism, and necessarily involves the servitude of the dependent majority of the population — a servitude which radiates from the economic into the political and cultural fields.

For no State, however shrewd and honourable those who manage its affairs may be, can effectively safeguard the interest of the non-possessing majority of those who depend for their very lives upon access to and use of the monopolies, if the legal system of the country recognizes private property in these monopolies, with the owners' unrestricted right to do what they like with their own.

Moral and economic causes therefore combine to induce latter-day human beings to repudiate — as far as the aforesaid monopolies are concerned — the capitalist economic law that 'private property is sacred'.

Basically different, on principle, is ownership of the goods whose quantity can be augmented at will — ordinary commodities of whatever kind. Their ownership (and we shall see later this applies also to money) does not create any such 'economic power over the non-possessing', for these latter are not dependent upon goods that are at any time augmentable, and therefore do not become the dependents of the 'private owners' of such goods.

### C. Capitalist Economic Form

Lastly the war [of 1914-1918], through the fierce industrialization that occurred, had a disastrous effect upon the bodily and still more upon the mental health of the Germans. Doubts concerning the 'victory of machinery' were intensified by the results of the rationalization that took place during the post-war period, producing huge industrial undertakings — and vast bodies of unemployed.

Not without effect, moreover, were the results of the renewed contact with nature which the men at the fighting front had had in the trenches, the youngsters in their hiking leagues, and the unemployed in their allotments, thanks to which, in industrial life afterwards, they all began to ask themselves whether the great town with its brick-built dens, the murderous giant factories with their conveyers, really provided worth-while conditions during the brief span between cradle and grave.

The feelings of the masses turned away more and more from the capitalist economic forms of industrialization, the tentacular towns, and manufacturing technique, and made the dispossessed more and more insistent in their demand for new forms.

Therein a genuinely conservative repudiation found utterance — a repudiation of the tendency to overvalue the technical and other recent acquirements of civilization. Herein we have an important distinction from Marxism, which in these matters, likewise, shows its mental kinship to liberalism. (We see signal examples of this in Russia, where Marxist panegyrics on industrial development are in high favour, and where the recent 'Stakhanoff Movement' reminds us so much of certain features of early-liberal capitalism.)

To the liberal (and Marxian) ideal of a boundless increase in production and consumption we contrapose the conservative (and socialist) ideal of a thoughtful and cheerful existence, which naturally requires as its foundation a sufficient supply of the necessaries of life, but seeks and finds its main fulfilment in very different values.

The first thing that emerges from the foregoing discussions is the reason why the economic policy, the economic law, and the economic form of capitalism are in the throes of a crisis from which no exit can be found; but we are also introduced to the germs of the trend and the kind of economic policy, economic laws, and economic form that will characterize German socialism.

### 2. ECONOMIC POLICY OF GERMAN SOCIALISM

Arising very urgently out of the collapse of world economy, world trade, and the gold standard, come the demands of German socialism for autarchy, a State monopoly of foreign trade, and a currency standard of our own.

#### A. Autarchy

Autarchy, self-sufficiency, i.e. adequate domestic sources for the supply of raw materials, is a necessary antecedent to the satisfaction of the main demand of a socialist national economy — the safeguarding of the food, clothing, and shelter of the community. It is also the necessary antecedent to national freedom and popular cultural development, as is plainly shown to the German people by the issue of the world war. With regard to food-supply, autarchy must be absolute, whereas in the case of our minimal cultural requirements it can be and will be relative. We already have the bulk of the conditions. With the necessary improvements, our agriculture and stock-raising could supply a sufficiency of food for the German people. The most important raw materials that are lacking (cotton, oil, and rubber), can in part be replaced by such substitutes as artificial silk and flax and in part by synthetic products.

Efforts to make our national economy independent of the rest of the world will be facilitated by simplifying the lives of our fellow-countrymen. Under the capitalist system a great many 'daily needs' are artificially developed by advertisement. Simplifying life would not mean a 'relapse into barbarism', for culture is not dependent upon luxury or upon the gratification of needlessly created wants. In a true fellowship no one would make a to-do about the satisfaction of such needs while any of his fellow-countrymen were going hungry from lack of work.

Thus the stress that is laid upon promoting the idea of autarchy needs certain restrictions — but still more does it need an important amplification.

National autarchy cannot and must not be the last aim of a socialist economic policy, for we are not concerned with a Spartan ideal, but with a Dionysiac ideal, in the profoundest sense of the term. Consequently this national autarchy can only be a transitional phase — though the present international situation makes us suppose that it will be the terminal phase of German socialism. Not through our own will, but under stress of circumstances — and it seems undesirable that one nation should blame another for these circumstances.

European autarchy, however, is here deliberately advocated as the necessary economic policy of German socialism, since this is essential to the maintenance of the level of European culture and civilization, and can be shown to be possible if there is a suitable adjustment of agricultural and industrial capacities for production and consumption. Nothing but the establishment and safeguarding of European autarchy can make it safe to carry on a luxury-trade with other parts of the world without endangering the existence of Europe. For the very reason that European autarchy is an aim of German socialism, and for the very reason that extant political and economic data are still obstacles to the reaching of this aim, the national autarchy of German socialism is an indispensable antecedent thereto.

### B. State Monopoly of Foreign Trade

So far as import of raw materials or luxuries seems necessary or desirable, the German people will export some of its own wares in exchange for the requisites, exporting the produce either of a natural monopoly (potash, chemicals) or of an artificial monopoly (electro-plate, expensive machinery, etc.).

The exchange will not be effected in accordance with the arbitrary wishes of the individual producers, but in accordance with a plan drafted to suit the needs of the State, and this will involve the existence of a State monopoly of foreign trade. Such a State monopoly will not (as does the Russian) aim at itself conducting the foreign trade, but will merely supervise, and give licences for export to such persons as may need them.

Once more it is necessary to distinguish between what may be the terminal situation of German socialism, and what may be aimed at beyond it.

In what will probably be the situation of German socialism to begin with, a national monopoly of foreign trade will be urgently required. Not merely will the natural opposition of international capitalism render indispensable this concentration of all the forces of the German national economy, but the monopoly will also suit the needs of a planned economy, without which a socialist economy is impossible.

Inasmuch as even after European autarchy has been established, the internal structures of the various national economies will differ, when this later condition is reached German socialism will not be able to dispense with the monopoly of foreign trade.

The fact that there will only be a monopoly in granting licences to trade will make it easy to adapt matters to the various requirements of intra-European and overseas trade.

Above all it will safeguard and turn to useful account those incommunicable experiences in foreign trade which cannot be acquired by any bureaucratic apparatus.

### C. A Currency Standard of Our Own

Abandonment of the international gold standard will be an essential preliminary to autarchy, for so long as the foreign world can have any influence on our currency (which is the 'blood' of economic life), no really independent national economy is possible. As regards the practicability of our having a currency standard of our own, it might be enough to point to the German rentenmark or to the Russian chervonets. But so great is the interest taken in currency questions that it seems expedient to make a few general remarks upon the problem of money and the problem of the gold standard.

The preponderant part that money plays in contemporary economic life is due to the circumstance that, in addition to fulfilling the tasks of being a medium of exchange and a standard of value, money is also a commodity, being in most countries dependent on gold, a commodity which is privileged over all other commodities by having assigned to it by law a fixed value. This peculiar commodity-character of money as dependent on gold, and the concentration of the extant supplies of gold in the hands of the great financiers, enable these in all States where gold is current coin, or at least the standard of currency, to exert a decisive influence upon the economic life of the States concerned, an influence whose danger has repeatedly been disclosed by the events of post-war political life. The commodity money-gold has, moreover, a peculiar quality which attaches to no other commodity, namely the power of increasing itself through interest accruing while it lies idle and its owner does nothing at all.

This quality of gold is not natural but artificial. The natural purpose of money is to facilitate exchange. Money is (1) a means of exchange, (2) a measure of value. Since in a large and complicated economic unit, barter becomes impracticable, the producer sells his goods, receiving in exchange, not goods of corresponding value, but a 'certificate', a 'token', of the value of what he has sold. He accepts this token being confident that therewith he will be able to buy a corresponding amount of other goods. He does not primarily wish to exchange commodities for money, but commodities for commodities. He will only be able to do this if the goods he wants are already obtainable or will soon be obtainable in the market. Confidence in the purchasing power of the monetary certificate or token which he accepts, gives this token its value, makes the token 'current coin' (or current notes). All currency is therefore sustained by the confidence of the owners of the current coin and of the mass of goods ready for exchange. If the current coin is faced by a suitable quantity of goods, the stability of the currency is ensured. When goods are scarce, money depreciates, for a fixed amount of money will buy less: when there is a glut, money appreciates, for the same amount of money will buy more. Only in a circumscribed economic system, where the circulation of money and the circulation of goods are not exposed to the influence of outside forces, is it possible to make sure that the quantity of money and the quantity of goods shall be in an appropriate relation each to the other. By the State monopoly of foreign trade we shall be able to prevent any outside forces from exerting undue influence upon the quantity of marketable goods, and by having a currency standard of our own we shall be enabled to exert a decisive influence upon the circulation of money.

It is necessary here to remind the reader of the difference between the immediate national aim in these matters, and the ultimate aim of the United States of Europe.

However urgent it may be for German socialism to establish a currency of its own, this must be supplemented by establishing, within the European economic system we aspire to (brought about no matter how), a supra-national currency available throughout the joint region.

Various practical considerations seem to indicate that the stable Swiss franc can and will become the supra-national currency, this giving new tasks to a Swiss banking system, under general European control.

3. ECONOMIC LAW OF GERMAN SOCIALISM

*A. Private Property?*

The transformation of economic policy by the establishment of autarchy, a State monopoly of foreign trade, and a currency standard of our own — subsumed under the comprehensive term of a 'planned economy', is today regarded as necessary by numerous groups in Germany and elsewhere in Europe. But this theoretical recognition of 'planned economy' will remain sterile so long as these groups still cling to the prevailing capitalist economic law which decrees that 'private property is sacred'.

With the utmost possible emphasis, therefore, the conservative revolutionist must at this point insist upon (as indispensable preliminary to a genuine and effective planned economy) the abrogation of the prevailing economic law of private property.

One who takes his stand upon the maintenance of private property in land, the raw materials that lie beneath the surface of the land, and the means of production in general, is not only repudiating German socialism, but is also defending what will make a planned economy impossible — no matter how ardently in theory he may desire it.

This follows without more ado from the very nature of the owner's claim that he has the right 'to do what he likes with his own', the claim which forms the core of the legal notion of 'private property'. So long as the owner of land, the raw materials that lie beneath the surface of the land, and the means of production in general, can do what he pleases with his 'property'; so long as the peasant can cultivate his fields or not as he prefers, the owner of a coalmine have the coal mined or not as he likes best, the factory owner have his factory working or idle at his own sweet will — just so long is a planned economy impossible. (To say nothing about the privilege of the owner to sell his property to a foreign individual, corporation, or State, which would be fatal to the organization of a German planned economy.)

For these reasons therefore, as well as for the moral reasons that have already been specified, the abolition of private property in land, the raw materials that lie beneath the surface of the land, and the means of production, is the main demand of German socialism, and the presupposition to a planned national economy.

The same demand is made by all Marxians, and to this extent they are socialists, though the carrying into effect and the fruitfulness of their demand have been hindered and will be hindered by their liberal alienism. I consider it expedient to dwell upon the identity of demand in this respect as between the international Marxians and the German socialists, this being a prelude to insisting, as regards constructive methods, upon the difference between Marxism and German Socialism.

## B. 'Entail'[1]

This difference is based upon our (conservative) view of the nature of (German) human beings.

Biological and historical experience precludes the possibility of any change in human nature, and even of an intention to change it. Our political task is therefore to study human nature as it actually exists in its German stamp, and to allow for that nature in our economic and social institutions. We must not try to force an economic theory upon Germans, but, on the contrary, we must

---

[1] This term is not here quite identical with the specifically English use of the word 'entail', but we know of no other possible term for the rendering of the German *Erblehen* We therefore use it in quote marks  Its meaning will soon become plain to careful readers. A conceivable alternative term would be 'usufruct', but this lacks the 'atmosphere' of 'entail'.--*Translators' Note.*

deduce an economic theory from the nature of Germans, and, more particularly, we must then formulate an economic system under which Germans can live and develop. (If, in what follows, we deal exclusively with 'Germans', this is merely to restrict our field, and not from any overweening presumption.)

First of all, then, let me insist that the German has a longing for his own peculiar style, for independence, for delight in responsibility and joy in creation. The lack of possibilities for satisfying this longing constitutes the tap-root of the homelessness, the discontent, the purposelessness of the existence of the latter-day German. He suffers, in a word, from the proletarian character of his life, from his lack of possessions, from the hopeless prospect of his old age, and from the dependence of his present.

To deproletarianize the Germans must therefore be the main task of German socialism.

This deproletarianization is only possible by finding possessions for every German. Nothing but possessions of his own can give that independence of thought and development, that stamp of creative energy, and that experience of the sense of responsibility which can really and truly satisfy a German.

This brings us to two apparently contradictory demands of German socialism:

(1) No German shall any longer have private property in land, the raw materials that lie beneath the surface of the land, and the means of production in general;

(2) Every German shall have possessions in these same things.

The escape from the apparent contradiction between these two fundamental demands of German socialism can be made by something which we were the first to advocate — the introduction of 'entail'.

The nation, that is to say the whole body of the German people, the community at large, is the sole owner of the land, the raw materials that lie beneath the surface of the land, and the means of production in general, the right of exploiting these being assigned to individual Germans in 'entail' according as they may be capable and worthy of it.

To make this demand intelligible we must briefly distinguish between 'private property' [Eigentum] and 'possession' [Besitz].

To have a thing as one's 'private property' means that one can do what one likes with it — can sell it, injure it, or destroy it at will.

To have 'possession' of a thing means usufruct, that one is entitled to use the thing, to exploit it, but subject to the will and supervision of another, the substantial 'owner', whose 'private property' it is.

The proprietor of the entire German national economy will henceforward be no one other than the community at large, the whole nation. But the nation, or its organizational form the State, will not run this economy itself. It will hand the national economy over, fragmented and in 'entail', for exploitation by German individuals or German groups.

This watchword of 'entail' forms the core of German socialism.

Nothing but 'entail' will render possible that combination of general welfare with private advantage which is another of the aims of German socialism, since it conforms with the inalienable requirements of human nature.

Intolerable to the highly developed individualism of the Germans (and doubtless of other Europeans) would be any economic or social system that should run counter to a German's personal initiative or restrict his freedom. The brief interlude of the Hitler System will make no change here.

The fatal defect of the capitalist economic system has been that its increasing monopolization and bureaucratization of the masses has for them done away with the possibility of their having lives of their own, of advancing, of acquiring possessions. This 'proletarianization', with its terrible economic phenomena and its ghastly cultural defects, cannot be overcome by universalizing a proletarian lack of possessions. Deproletarianization is absolutely essential to the cure of this cancer of our time: I mean the assignment of possessions to all working members of the community, either as individuals or associated in groups.

This will be rendered possible by 'entail', which for centuries was the legalized form of the German and European economic system, and which, in its fruitful tension between the community spirit and the individual will, represents the German and western way of managing affairs.

### C. Repudiation of State Socialism

This systematized method of 'entail' further involves an emphatic rejection of any form of State capitalism, euphemistically termed State socialism.

The need for the repudiation must be thoroughly explained, all the more because not only the Marxians but many sections of non-Marxians who are working for a

147

'national planned economy' aspire towards State capitalism — or, as they prefer to say, State socialism.

In so far as this would involve the transfer of all ownership rights to the community, as represented by the
State, it is in perfect harmony with the aims of German
socialism.

But when we come to the carrying on of enterprises by
the State or its organs, the German socialists are passionately opposed to such a method, because thereby
mental deproletarianization, the development of creative
energy, and the encouragement of delight in responsibility would be even more impaired than they are in the
private capitalist system — to say little of the fact that
those who did the work would be even more under the
thumb of their employer.

So well do I know from personal experience what a
destructive effect bureaucratic control has upon the
individuality of the workers, and, on the other hand,
what a craving for independence the German peasants
and the members of the German middle class have, that
I cannot but regard with disfavour any scheme which
would kill this craving for independence by the blight of
bureaucracy.

To my way of thinking the chief curse of proletarian
life is the lack or the perpetual suppression of a longing
for independence, and I therefore believe it to be the
chief aim of mental deproletarianization to provide
independence for the urban operatives rather than to
undermine the independence of peasants and members
of the middle class by proletarianizing them.

We have furthermore to consider the increased
subordination of all 'hands', financially, socially, politi-

cally, and personally, when the State, besides being their employer, will be their only court of appeal. Under private capitalism the State (since the worker who has a complaint to lodge is anyhow one subject much like another, being a taxpayer and a soldier) must always be fairly impartial in its attitude towards the employer, and this benefits the worker.

But under State capitalism there is no such impartiality since employer and State are one and the same person, one and the same authority.

I know that the revolutionary Marxians try to invalidate this argument by pointing out that their 'State' is the proletarian dictatorship, in which there can be no antagonism between employee and State. However, so long as a bureaucracy exists, there is no genuine proletarian dictatorship, but only the rule of a class, the official class, over the great mass of the working people, who are far more effectively subjected to the class dominion of the bureaucracy than today under capitalism they are subjected to the class dominion of the owners of the means of production.

Decisively in favour of our 'entail' plan is the popular belief that it is a million times more contributory to the people's welfare that there should be a thousand independent peasants than a thousand agricultural workers in State employ; in other words that the crucial aim of German socialism must be to make the number of economically independent persons as large as is the number of citizens who actually exist inspired with a will to independence.

The repudiation of State capitalism and State socialism is one of the most marked characteristics of German socialism. Herein German socialism gives expression both to a genuinely conservative scepticism of organization and to the popular dislike for bureaucracy; and it also avows its faith in individuality, which is threatened just as much by mass rule as by party dictatorship. (We shall return to this when we come to discuss the State.)

The fascists and the communists rival one another in glorifying the State, in suppressing economic and personal independence, in unduly extolling power and the successes of organization, of decrees, of planning, and — as a last requisite — the police.

It is precisely in the economic field that the German socialists deliberately aim at the utmost independence and autonomy of all fit members of the population; and in their system those who do not achieve individual economic autonomy will, by combining to form co-operatives, acquire a considerable measure of that independence which is the only soil where firm characters can grow.

To this popular (non-economic) outlook the German socialists purposely subordinate all such views as 'what pays best', 'the greatest good of the greatest number', etc.


## 4. ECONOMIC FORM OF GERMAN SOCIALISM

The popular outlook likewise dictates our aims as regards the economic form of German socialism.

Those who understand that life in our huge tentacular towns is a danger to the human race cannot fail to regard systematic de-urbanization as urgently required for the sake of the people. De-urbanization will also be a logical consequence of the establishment of autarchy and the introduction of 'entail' as regards peasant farming, since both will make it necessary that Germany should be agrarianized once more.

This re-agrarianization of Germany will be supported from the towns by a far-reaching policy of land-settlement, which will mainly take the form of 'marginal settlements'.

Here it becomes appropriate to mention in passing that systematic de-urbanization in conjunction with a marginal settlement policy will be of the utmost importance to the defence of our country, inasmuch as thereby the risks to the industrial centres from aviation attacks with poison-gas and incendiary or explosive bombs will be greatly reduced through the dispersion of motive force that has now been rendered possible by the distant transmission of gas and electricity and by the local use of internal combustion engines.

The utilization of these recent discoveries will further make it possible to fulfil the demand of German socialism that industry should be decentralized for its own sake, and that the excessive industrialization of German economic life should be counteracted.

To the liberal capitalist and liberal Marxian ideal of modern mammoth factories producing vast quantities of goods, we should contrapose the conservative ideal of a full and free life, so that it will be the task of a responsible government to create the economic and social conditions essential to the realization of such an ideal.

No sane conservative will admit that it is reactionary to shatter, as far as may be desirable, the idols of mechanical technique. It is assuredly time for Germans to end the tyranny of technique, to overthrow the dominion of the machine, and to make technique and the machine once more servants instead of masters — for their domination has been an unmitigated curse.

Already, in the subsection on Capitalist Economic Form (pp. 135 and foll.), I have referred to the new attitude which German socialism adopts towards the problem of 'man and economic life'.

Most emphatically do we reject the capitalist (and Marxian) creed that man is sent into the world 'in order to work'. The Song of Labour is a capitalist device for the training of diligent slaves, and the same characterization applies to both the fascist and the communist glorification of labour, whose sole aim really is to inculcate diligence upon the slaves of the State.

The conservative revolutionist regards labour as nothing but the means for the maintenance of life, an instrument which can only transcend narrow limits in the higher form of 'creation'.

Consequently industrial work with its murderous monotony must somehow enable the individual worker to find a chance for 'creation' outside his daily round of toil, i.e. this daily round must not claim more than a fraction of his life. (But at the same time as much attention as possible must always be paid to the 'spiritualization' of daily labour itself.)

In view of the vast productive powers of modern German factories, etc., there is nothing utopian in the idea that various branches of industry can produce a sufficiency by winter work alone or mainly, so that the workers engaged in these branches will be left free during the summer for their own 'creative' work, for learning to know their fatherland better, the world at large, and what not.

The disintegration of titanic enterprises and a healthier estimate of the role of machinery will give their stamp to this new life, even as increasing joy will promote new sociability and foster true culture.

These ideas will be admirably rounded off when the spiritual leadership of the New Germany no longer has its headquarters established in one of the nerve-destroying giant towns, but in a new and carefully chosen capital of the Reich. For historical and other reasons, Goslar or Ratisbon would seem admirably fitted for this purpose.

Later historians will recognize how overwhelmingly strong are the arguments in favour of such a conservative choice, and will agree that the governmental capital of a country ought not to be in one of its great industrial towns. They will point to the examples of Versailles and Paris, of Potsdam and Berlin; and, outside Europe, to Washington and Kyoto as against New York and Tokyo.

## 5. AGRICULTURE

### A. *The Coming System*

The object of agriculture is to make sure that the community will be fed.

The land available for the use of the community is owned exclusively by the nation, for it was not by any individual but by the community at large that the land was acquired, by battle or by colonization on the part of the community, and by the community it has been defended against enemies.

The community as owner puts the land at the disposal

of the nation in the form of 'entails' to those able and willing to use them for husbandry and stock-raising.

This 'entailing' will be undertaken by the self-governing corporation of the local peasant-councils (see below, Chapter Three, 5 *B*, Vocational Councils, pp. 192 and foll.) and the appropriate circle president will merely act on the instructions of that corporation.

The size of the farms will be limited in accordance with the local qualities of the land: the maximum being determined by the principle that no one may hold in 'entail' more land than he is able to farm unaided; and the minimum being determined by the principle that the landholder must have enough land to provide, not only food for self and family, but a superfluity by the disposal of which he will be able to obtain clothing and shelter for self and family.

The maximum limitation will result in freeing large quantities of land for settlement by peasants, particularly in Eastern Germany. This peasant settlement is all the more necessary because the existence of an abundance of peasants thus settled on their own farms furnishes the best guarantee for the maintenance of public health and public energy.

The landholder who thus receives a farm on 'entail' will pledge himself to manage this farm for the best advantage of the community and to use his utmost endeavours to make sure that the land shall be farmed to supply the food of the community. He will therefore have to pay a land-tax, a tithe-rent, to the community. This will be payable in kind, the amount being fixed in accordance with the area and quality of the land. No other taxes will be payable by the peasant.

Should the holder of an 'entail' die, the farm will pass to a son able and willing to carry it on. If there are no male children available, the 'entail' will revert to the community, and will be reallotted by the local peasants' council.

In the event of bad farming, an 'entail' will also revert to the community, the decision upon this matter resting with the local self-governing body (peasants' council) in agreement with the State (represented by the circle president).

The introduction of 'entail' into German agriculture will be in such manifest conformity with German tradition and with the right and necessary ideas of peasant possessorship, that neither psychological nor material difficulties are likely to ensue.

Even the Hitler System, which had not attempted any radical attack upon capitalism, was compelled, upon pressure from the German peasants, to introduce a measure that was based in some degree upon the same ideas.

But the Patrimonial Farm Law of the Hitler regime differs from our 'entail' plan in the most essential respects.

(1) It leaves the entire capitalist system in being. For this reason the patrimonial farm peasant has great difficulty in securing credit, since, in view of the nature of his tenancy, the capitalists will not lend him money.

(2) The extant fiscal system levies taxes in money from the patrimonial farm peasants, who can only pay their dues by getting into debt.

(3) Old mortgage liabilities remain, as well as other debts, and to pay the interest on these (let alone clearing

off the principal) is even more impossible to a patrimonial farm peasant than to a freeholder.

(4) It extends only to a portion of the peasantry, and has therefore created three kinds of agricultural entrepreneurs: peasants whose holdings are so small as to be unviable; middle and great peasants who are tenant-farmers; and great landowners who run their estates on purely capitalist lines.

(5) It protects the great landowners who, sheltering behind the Patrimonial Farm Law, can avoid having their estates divided up, and thus frustrate their younger sons' hopes of attaining at least a peasant's independence.

(6) It is an instrument controlled by the State and the party bureaucracy, not a method of peasant self-government.

(7) It knows nothing of the cancellation of tenure which the local government can effect in cases of bad farming, nor yet of reversion of the land to the community when the family becomes extinct in the male line.

## B. Management of the Transition

When we compare this coming system with the present one, in order to discover how the transition can best be managed, we find first of all that the majority of German peasants will remain in possession of their farms.

For of the 5,096,533 farms in Germany (census of 1925) only 18,668 were of the size of 500 acres or more. All the others are peasant farms, and would remain such under the new system.

Indeed, properly speaking they would first become peasant farms under the new system. The transformation of 'privately owned farms' into 'entailed possessions' would necessarily involve the cancellation of all mortgages, land held as an 'entail' under the new system being by hypothesis unmortgageable. The transformation would free the peasants from their burden of debt, and would make it impossible for them to get into debt again. The new (really Old-Germanic) organization of land tenure would make the man who is now enslaved by having to pay interest into a free peasant.

This complete liberation of German agriculture from debt, as a necessary consequence of the proposed 'entail' system, carrying with it the impossibility of the burden of debt ever being renewed, is of decisive importance, first, to promote both psychologically and materially the acceptance of German socialism by the peasants; and, secondly, to make our agriculture a paying concern for all time.

For in this way German socialism would justly present itself to the peasant as the redeemer, coming to deliver him for evermore from the claws of the mortgagees, the bankers, and the tax-gatherers.

To save the creditors from ruin, and in this way to avert a convulsion in the capitalist money-market, the sums owing on mortgage would be converted into non-interest-bearing bonds payable by the Mortgage Cancellation Department, a three-per-cent sinking-fund being arranged by the Agricultural Tenants' Redemption Scheme.

No less important, as the system gets into working order, will be the disappearance of the taxes now demanded from the peasants by the State, in place of which there will be one general annual payment of the 'tithe',

so that there will be no possibility of the peasant possessions becoming once more burdened with debt.

The danger to the State that there may be variations
in the revenue from the tithes, and the danger to the
peasants of there being localized failure of the crops, will
be obviated by the solidarization of the peasantry of the
circle and the province. (Whereby at the same time will
be established the necessary community of material
interests among the peasants — a community that will
make the working of the peasants' councils stable and
effective.

### C. Great Landed Estates

The subdivision of the great landed estates will be
fundamental to the re-agrarianization of Germany,
which is one of the aims of German socialism.

The 18,688 big farms in Germany, of a size of 500
acres and upwards each, utilize more than 16.7 % — or
if we take in all farms of 250 acres and upwards, more
than 20 % — of the land suitable for agricultural purposes. Even stronger than this moral argument is the
urgent need for the provision of more peasant farms,
since nothing else can prevent the second and third sons
of our peasants from drifting into the towns.

The objection that such expropriation of the great
landed estates would be unjust is invalid, seeing that
what remained for the former owners, who would become
'entail' farmers, would be completely freed from debt;
and, further, compensation could be paid by the Mortgage Cancellation Department.

The main objection advanced against dividing-up the
great landed estates into independent peasant farms (an

objection voiced both by Marxians and by capitalists) is the alleged indispensability of large-scale farming to the supply of a sufficiency of cereals to the great towns.

This argument is based upon various considerations, some of which are still sound today but will be overruled tomorrow, when the proposed de-urbanization of great industries will have markedly reduced the population of our towns — a movement which will be reinforced by administrative and military defensive measures.

Besides, the systematic intensification of agriculture by the spread of market-gardening will in any case involve a structural change such as we see in Denmark and Holland, and this presupposes the partition of the great landed estates.

Finally the inclusion of the south-east, the granary of Europe, in the economic system of Central Europe, in conjunction with the other general aims of the European Federation, will inevitably liberate Germany from the need for producing cereals 'at all hazards' — a need which would impair the chances for the establishment of a planful agricultural system in this part of the world.

It has already been pointed out that these changes will take time. Obviously, therefore, the partition of the great landed estates must be part of a general plan for agrarian reform that will look years ahead, making arrangements for the erection of the necessary farm-buildings and habitations, the choice of the young peasants who will run the new small farms, the provision of agricultural implements, live-stock, etc. Not least, the State will have to found in each province a number of model farms, as centres for the supply of seed, for stock-raising, and general agricultural progress. This development will facilitate the maintenance of the extant 'model farms' that have been established by progressive landowners, the personal services and peculiar skill of these being recognized and utilized by appointing them 'bailiffs of the domains'.

It is important to remember that the tithe-rent payable to the State can be paid in kind, and that this will save the peasants from the wasteful conversion of their produce into money, whereas the State will in a very simple way come into possession of a notable part of the harvest, which it will to some extent use directly as food-supply for the army, and to some extent put on the market as may seem desirable to regulate prices. (The salaries of officials, allowances to pensioners, etc., may be partly payable in kind.)

The transition from the capitalist agriculture of today to the socialist agriculture of tomorrow will thus be comparatively easy, because the German peasantry has an interest in escaping from the fleecing capitalist system, and in gaining and safeguarding a position in which the peasants will be free and independent.

## 6. INDUSTRY AND WHOLESALE TRADE

Industrial enterprises are fundamentally different from agricultural enterprises. Whereas an agricultural enterprise is mainly carried on by the work of an individual and his dependents, an industrial enterprise needs the collaboration of a manager or foreman and his staff of workers. The produce of agriculture varies with the soil and the climatic conditions; the produce of industry varies with the supply of raw materials and their

distribution. Raw materials are either supplied from the
sources within the country, such as coal deposits, ores,
etc., which are the property of the community, or else
they are procured by import (in Germany: oil, cotton.
and rubber). For the freedom and independence of a
national economy, it is essential that there should be (to
the extent previously explained) autarchy and a State
monopoly of foreign trade. In this way the State acquires
a decisive influence upon the supply of an industry with
raw materials, and it must be in a position to cope with
the requirements of production for use. Thus besides
the manager and his staff of workers there must be a
third party to the affair as representative of the community, and there are three factors concerned in any
industrial enterprise:

Manager; Staff of Workers; the State.

It is needful that we should have a clear idea of this
tripartition of interests that results from the very nature
of the industrial process, since therefrom are logically
derived the forms of possession, the management of
enterprise, and the distribution of profits, as envisaged
by German socialism.

German socialism emphatically repudiates a totalitarian claim on the part of any one of these three factors:
whereas capitalism makes a totalitarian claim on behalf
of the entrepreneur; fascism makes a totalitarian claim
on behalf of the State (a claim it has not so far been
possible to enforce in practice); and communism makes
a totalitarian claim on behalf of the workers.

As contrasted with the totalitarian claim of any one
factor, we have the notion of an equipoise throughout the
whole, and here (in current parlance) is manifested an

important distinction between liberalism and conservatism.

### A. *The Factory Fellowship*

Manager, staff of workers, and State are the three partners in any enterprise They constitute a factory fellowship.

The State, which in agriculture is the exclusive proprietor of the land, is equally, in an industrial enterprise, the exclusive proprietor of the concern. Through the instrumentality of the appropriate vocational council it assigns the work in fief to a manager who is competent and willing to undertake it. In return there will be payable to the State an impost (corresponding to the tithe payable by an agricultural enterprise), the amount of which will be assessed at regular intervals (5 or 10 years, let us say). These imposts, since, in conjunction with the tithes from agricultural enterprises, they must provide for State expenditure upon public affairs, will have priority over net profits, allowances for wear and tear, and reserves.

Management, possession, and profits are thus assigned in thirds to the manager, the staff of workers, and the State. The management decides about the world policy of the enterprise, settling the kind and quantity of goods to be produced, fixing the respective amounts payable for depreciation (wear and tear), reserve, and profit, and prescribing the wages to be paid.

Whilst the approved imposts from the works, in conjunction with the tithes from agriculture, are the returns payable to the State for safeguarding the public economy, the share of the State in the profits represents a variable

revenue which can be disbursed for special purposes.
(Current expenses: for administration, education, army,
etc.: extraordinary expenses; public buildings, canals,
power stations, etc.)

The manager derives his income from his share in
possession and profits, so that his economic position
turns upon the success or failure of the enterprise.
Success will depend upon his devoting his whole time
and capacity: and his share should, therefore, be comparatively large.

In virtue of his share in the possession of the enterprise,
every member of the working staff will draw a portion of
the profits, and will also receive wages suitable to his
achievements. The two together form the basis of his
economic self-maintenance.

The respective shares of the manager and the working
staff in the profits must be so apportioned that the
manager will be able to provide for his own living expenses and those of his family out of his share in the
profits and nothing more, whereas the worker's ordinary
expenditure will be defrayed out of his wages. The
manager's share in possession and profits must, therefore,
be comparatively large, whilst that of the individual
worker can be comparatively small. Furthermore it is
undesirable that the workers should have a large share
in the profits, for such copious profit-sharing may foster
a deleterious overdriving of the means of production and
the neglect of improvements that technical and hygienic
considerations render desirable.

It is also essential to remember that there should not be
any aim at large profits, since these are excluded by paying
due regard to the need for good wages and low prices.

The factory fellowships with their basis of fiefs thus resemble the agricultural enterprises with their basis of 'entails', but the former are substantially collective, whereas the latter are substantially individual in character.

Of especial importance are three primary qualities of this new form of industrial enterprise:

(1) There will come into being, in contradistinction to the extant 'class' of capitalists, an 'estate' of managers which, regardless of wealth or origin, will constitute a functional aristocracy that, thanks to the very methods of its selection, may be said to be made up of 'captains of industry' or 'commissioned officers of economic life'.

(2) The dispossessed 'class' of proletarians will vanish, its place being taken by an 'estate' of fully privileged workers, directly and indirectly participating in and therefore interested in their 'workshop'. They will no longer be the objects of economy, but its subjects.

(3) The relations between State and economic life will be radically altered. The State will not be the 'night-watchman and policeman' of capitalism, nor will it be a dictator whose bureaucracy cracks the whip that drives the workers to the bench and spurs them at their tasks; but it will be trustee of the consumers, and as such it will have much influence, but only within and beside the self-determination of the working producers, namely of the manager (who may be a plurality) and the staff of workers (consisting in appropriate proportions of clerical and other intellectual workers, on the one hand, and manual operatives, on the other).

## B. Contrast to Capitalism and Marxism

It seems desirable to give a brief account of the basic distinction between the watchwords of German socialism in these matters and those of capitalism. on the one hand, Marxism. on the other.

### 1. DISTINCTION FROM CAPITALISM

*a.* There is no private property in the means of production. They can neither be bought nor sold, so that even though there may be persons who possess large quantities of commodities or money ('wealth' in this sense being both possible and permissible), nothing like 'capitalism' can come into existence.

*b.* The staff of workers and the State are equally privileged partners with the manager, who is not a 'capitalist', but merely a fief-holder.

*c.* The need for economic and systematic production is enforced upon the manager because his partners outnumber him.

*d.* Every German citizen is one of the joint possessors of the entire German economy.

### 2. DISTINCTION FROM MARXISM

*a.* The personal initiative of the responsible managers is preserved, but it is incorporated into the needs of the community.

*b.* Within the systematically planned management of the whole national economy by the State (organically safeguarded by the equal third of influence which the State has in every industrial enterprise) the wholesome rivalry of the individual enterprises is maintained.

*c.* The treatment of State and economic enterprise, that is to say of official and industrial manager, on an equal footing is avoided; so is the arbitrary power of the State which deprives the worker of his rights.

*d.* Everyone engaged in an enterprise is, in virtue of his being part-possessor as a citizen, one of the immediate and influential possessors of his enterprise, his 'workshop', and can exert this possessive right in full measure on the supervisory council of the concern.

The form of the factory fellowship, founded upon the legal idea of the fief, and vivified by the great self-governing body of the workers' and employees' councils, on the one hand, the industrial and trades' councils, on the other, constitutes the new economic system of German socialism, which is equally remote from western capitalism and eastern bolshevism, and nevertheless complies with the requirements of large-scale industry.

### C. Management of the Transition

Although the content and the form of German socialism are so strikingly different from those of the contemporary capitalist economic system, the technical management of the transition from one to the other will be comparatively easy — provided always that the political question of the change in the economic law has been overcome.

The simplest way will be to transform all industrial and trading enterprises that employ a considerable amount of labour-power into joint-stock companies, for the tripartition of possessorship and the corresponding subdivision of control and profits will be easy enough to arrange.

The 'shares' will, of course, be very different from those of the extant joint-stock companies, for they will be real portions, inalienable because of their fief-character, neither saleable nor pledgeable—non-negotiable in fact, belonging exclusively to the assignee.

The extent to which present 'owners' can become fief-holders will turn upon their achievements as effective managers of the enterprise in which they hold shares and upon their attitude towards the German Revolution. The formation of an 'estate' of managers is no less incumbent upon German socialism than the formation of an officers' corps was incumbent upon Prussia — an analogy of profound significance.

The unified representation of the State in the national economic life as a whole (a representation fundamentally distinct from the fascist regulation of economic life) will secure the lasting organic joint leadership of economic life by the State, without resulting in forcible intervention on the part of insufficiently skilled officials. More especially it will ensure the systematic de-urbanization of industry, in conjunction with its requisite unification and simplification, as well as the permanent control of production, wages, and prices. All this will grow organically from within, elaborated by experts, and unceasingly adjusted by the wills of the working staffs and the managers.

Thus the transformation of profit-making industry and trade into socialist industry and trade, working for use instead of profit, will be comparatively simple, because it will conform with the interests of the community, the workers, and even the managers whenever these are of sterling quality.

The most frequent objection is that our method of transition will render it possible for 'capitalists' to come into existence once more, or will perhaps actually leave them in being.

This objection overlooks the radical difference between a capitalist and a business-manager (entrepreneur), and especially does it forget that 'capitalism', that is to say economic power based upon monopoly-goods, cannot arise under the new conditions. No matter how much money a man may have, he will not be able to buy portions of an enterprise (the sometime 'shares'), which can now be held only in fief.

This becomes peculiarly plain when we consider how the monetary and banking system will be run under socialist control.

Except during the time of transition, when indubitably the needs of the situation will demand a (postponed) fixing of maximum and minimum incomes, the acquirement and possession of money will be limited by what work a man can do, and by that alone. Thereby the standard of life will be as much differentiated as human nature demands. (Of course a strict legal control of inheritance will play its part.) But the decisive point is that, under the conditions that will prevail, even the ownership of vast sums of money cannot lead to 'capitalism', because, although commodities of the kind that can be multiplied as much as you please are purchasable to any amount, monopolies such as land, the raw materials that lie beneath its surface, and the means of production in general, are not purchasable at all.

Consequently interest will still be obtainable for money, but with two important restrictions. The Reichsbank, which issues banknotes, is a State institution, and determines what the official rate of interest shall be, and by this rate the great banks (which will have the ordinary character of professional corporations, unless it has been

thought expedient to have them taken over by the State
will have to abide, with an additional allowance for expenses. On the other hand, the small banks and local
credit institutions will have more latitude in this matter
of the rate of interest. But credit will have to be granted
without any concrete security, so that it will be a purely
personal matter of notes-of-hand. There can be no mort-
gaging of land, factories, or business undertakings of any
kind, since they will all be national property assigned for
usufruct as 'entails' or fiefs.

The increased importance of private and local credit
institutes will, however, revive the private bankers of the
old days, and this will be 'good for trade'; advantageous
to the economic system as a whole. Owing to the
increased risk to the money thus lent on personal security
alone, 'interest slavery' having been done away with by
making mortgages impossible, the present objection to
'incomes made without trouble or labour' will cease to
exist.

Finally, this elastic way of treating the money and
interest problem will facilitate the practical testing of the
latest monetary theories, whose general application by
the community would involve excessive — and needless —
risk.

## 7. HANDICRAFT AND RETAIL TRADE

Under the caption of handicrafts and retail trade come
the various independent petty undertakings in which
there are no more workers (mostly styled 'apprentices',
'pupils', or 'assistants') than can have a reasonable
expectation of some day becoming independent themselves.

These handicraft enterprises and petty establishments for retail trade are fundamentally different from the factory fellowships. Whereas in a factory fellowship the success of the concern, and therewith the weal or woe of every one of the workers engaged in it, does not depend upon individuals but on the associated labour of all, the welfare of an independent handicraft enterprise depends upon the personality of the 'boss'. In a factory fellowship, problems are jointly decided by its three sections, the manager, the staff of workers, and the State; but, in the independent handicraft enterprise the boss decides 'on his own'. He is solely responsible for what is done. In a socialist economy this amount of personal freedom is only conceivable if there are leagues which organize the individuals into a community. Such a league will federate the handicrafts or branches of retail trade into a guild.

### A. *The Guild* (or *Corporation*)

Handicraft enterprises, small shops, and also the liberal professions, will therefore be incorporated into guilds.

The State will grant the guilds certain rights over their members, and in return the guilds will undertake to collect from their members the contributions which will make up the lump sum due from each guild in the way of taxes to the State.

They will allot the right to practise a petty industry or trade by conceding to suitable persons the title of 'master', which can only be acquired by one who gives definite undertakings. The guild will insist upon work of a certain quality, and in that case will guarantee support to the guildsmen. It will decide how many apprentices each guildsman may take, etc.

170

These regulations will render it impossible for the guildsman to pursue his own interests ruthlessly, to make an improper use of his economic freedom, for he will have to subordinate his interests to the needs of the community.

It will be obvious that one who is employed in such a petty enterprise is not entitled to any share in its possession, profits, or management. Though apparently disadvantaged as compared with the members of the working staff of a great enterprise, this is because the position of the former as employed members is different. In reality they are nothing more than apprentices or pupils who know that in due time, when they have given proof of competence, they will become independent masters.

This presupposes that the possibilities for such advancement have been duly considered by the guild and the administration, working together, and bearing in mind the public demand for persons practising such crafts or professions. The granting of diplomas by the authorities will be subordinated to the growth of population, and the schools will have to guide their pupils in the choice of avocations. Especially does this apply to the liberal and academic professions.

Such inevitable encroachments upon individual liberty will be more than compensated by increasing security of livelihood and promotion; apart from the fact that the encroachments will not be the work of bureaucratic State officials, but will be made solely through the instruments of a system of self-government that will have to act within a framework prescribed by the State.

## B. *Management of the Transition*

Here the extant vestiges of the guilds and cooperatives will provide stepping-stones. The advantages to the independent handicraftsmen and the members of the middle class that will derive from the new vocational associations, from the fixing of maximum numbers, etc., will be so great that the apparent disadvantage of the official control of prices will be fully made good — all the more seeing that the associations will be established by self-governing bodies, and will only be subject to State supervision.

Of great importance in this connexion will be the abolition of the existing scale and method of taxation, in place of which the guild will pay a lump sum, collected by the guild from its members.

The transformation of the minor handicrafts and petty retail establishments into the guild system of German socialism will be all the easier because the German handicraftsmen and small traders have a vital interest in escaping the destruction with which they are threatened by the capitalist system, and thus maintaining their existence as independent artisans, small shopkeepers, etc.

For the sake of completeness I must point out that house-ownership comes within the category of 'goods which can be augmented in quantity as much as you please' (see above, pp. 134-5), and will therefore remain private property. The necessary adjustment of rents will be arranged for by seeing to it that municipalities and cooperative building societies of all kinds shall provide a sufficiency of new dwellings on behalf of the public welfare — always on the presupposition (applying to privately owned houses no less than to others; that land is not private property, but will merely be leased to the housecowner as a fief for a definite term of years. This fundamental principle will make sure that the State or the municipality (which in general will here be trustee for the State) shall have a decisive influence in the building market. Besides, the new way of dealing with banks and mortgages will make it easy to control the building-sites on which fantastic groundrents are now paid. Thus from the monetary side the building market will be made healthy once more.

## 8. COOPERATIVE SOCIETIES

One of the main objects of German socialism is to combine the personal egoism that is a necessary and useful part of our human equipment with advantage for the general welfare, much as the working of the engine propels an automobile.

This aim finds expression, for example, in the fact that a peasant's tenure of his farm is to be arranged with an eye to communal benefit. The surplus he produces by working harder will be 'tax-free'. Another and even more striking instance is that there will be no limit to the acquisition of commodities other than the natural limit to a man's working powers. Herein, once more, is a sharp distinction between German socialism and Marxian communism, for the latter only recognizes personal freedom in such matters within marked limits. But the decisive point is that however much money a man may possess, or however large a quantity of goods, these will not enable him to become an owner of land, its mineral resources, or the means of production — for they are only obtainable on 'entail'. (Apart altogether from the heavy inheritance tax which, except for a few taxes on luxuries, will be the only 'tax' of the old sort to remain.)

Although our picture of German socialism can be no more than a sketch, we can at least make it plain that the voluntary formation of producers' and consumers' co-operatives will be strongly encouraged by the State, which will be competent to encourage it through playing so active a part in all great enterprises.

Though it will be uncongenial to the nature of German socialism to introduce any kind of State coercion into economic life, this objection is neither theoretical nor un-conditional, but merely represents a practical inference from the German character.

The development of cooperatives will be an important supplement to German socialism, and the economic counterpart to political self-government. It need hardly be said that the individual will be free to enter or leave a cooperative at will, partly because none but voluntary members can be expected to work cordially in the organization, and partly because nothing should be done to diminish the friendly rivalry between cooperative and non-cooperative enterprise. From this outlook it may be taken as a matter of course that there should be no material favouring of the cooperatives by the State, except that the State will certainly encourage the educational activities of the cooperatives, and this will be especially valuable where agricultural cooperatives are concerned.

Ideologically considered, the future trade unions will be simply workers' cooperatives whose main task will be to promote vocational training and development; for the economic and political interests of the workers (and employees) will be best served, directly by the workers' councils (or employees' councils), and indirectly by the estates' chambers. (See below, pp. 197 and foll.)

I may take this opportunity of repeating that the German temperament is equally opposed to the disposition of western capitalism to ignore the rights of the community, and to the disposition of eastern bolshevism to ignore individual responsibility and to despise the creative will of the personality.

The economic system of German socialism is, therefore, no less hostile to eastern bolshevism than to western capitalism; and our socialists feel strongly akin to those forms of the Middle Ages that gave expression to our national peculiarities, and to the essentials of the German nature.

## 9. PUBLIC ASSISTANCE

Public assistance comprises care for those members of the community who are no longer in a position to gain their own livelihood.

The main significance of the term 'community' or 'commonwealth' is that no one who belongs to it shall have to endure the miseries of poverty. For the duties which every citizen owes to the community are also entail rights, being set off by the duties which the community owes to every citizen.

This principle implies the need for a comprehensive system of national insurance, covering childhood, unemployment, accident, old age, and death, supplemented by voluntary insurance.

In contrast with the existing methods, the whole complicated system of insurance and support would be replaced under socialism by a unified life insurance. Every citizen would thereby be insured in a way that would guarantee him a sufficiency whatever happened, and no matter whether he (or she) was temporarily or permanently unfitted. Every citizen, moreover, by paying a supplementary premium, would be able to secure in case of need an allowance supplementary to that provided by the national insurance scheme.

As a matter of organization this would mean that all private insurance companies would be fused into one comprehensive national insurance scheme which would be directly connected with the Reichsbank. The economy effected by sweeping away the intricate apparatus of the extant private insurance companies, and by putting an end to the earning of considerable profits by the stockholders in such companies, would greatly reduce the premiums.

Further, matters would be much simplified by having only one aim of insurance — to safeguard the supply of a sufficiency for maintenance to anyone who should become unfitted for earning a livelihood, whether temporarily or permanently, and by whatever cause.

Desires for individual variations in what is regarded as a minimum subsistence would be met by having different grades of insurance. The lowest grade would be compulsory, and the premiums would be automatically deducted from wages or salary. What supplementary premiums were thought advisable would be decided by people themselves, at their own risk and at their own responsibility.

In these circumstances under German socialism there would be no further possibility that any members of the community should go hungry, as they do today, or even (horrible to relate) actually starve to death.

Every German, man or woman, would then be freed from the dread of poverty in old age, which now, to many, is a source of unceasing anxiety and gloom.

# CHAPTER THREE

# THE GERMAN SOCIALIST STATE

## I. MATTERS OF PRINCIPLE

IN accordance with the organic conception that all institutions must be judged by the extent to which they favour organic life, we regard the State, not as something that stands above the community at large, but as nothing else than the organizational form of the people, the form that will ensure the fullest possible development of the organism known as the 'German people'. The State is not an end in itself, but something whose aim is (or should be) so to deal with the organism of the 'people' (or 'nation') that it may most effectively utilize all the energies that will enable the community to maintain itself as against other communities in the world.

It follows from this that the State is always determined by the peculiarities of the people. No people can take over intact the State-forms of another. When the form of the State is adapted to the peculiarities of the people of one country, our organic outlook makes it plain that this form of State cannot be perfectly adapted to the peculiarities of any other people. If, for instance, fascism is the form of State best suited to the Italian people (and the fact that the Italian people tolerates it makes this probable), then fascism cannot be the form of State best suited to the German people. The same considerations apply to the bolshevik form of State which prevails in Russia, which cannot possibly be the best form of State for the German people.

The State must originate out of the nature of the people; it should arrange the people's life, and reduce internal friction to a minimum, for then the outwardly directed energies will grow more powerful. The athlete who trains for some great achievement, who makes his nerves and muscles cooperate without friction, and who by the regular practice of graduated exercises also cultivates the mental powers of self-confidence and will-to-victory, is the model of an organism in prime condition. A team trained for success in some particular sport, such as football, is a community whose chances of victory depend on the same presupposition — the reducing of internal friction to a minimum, in order to secure the maximum output of well-directed energy.

This conception of the State as the best possible organization of the people involves the rejection on principle of the demigod role which all dictators and would-be dictators ascribe to the State, and implies the frank avowal of the 'people's State'. The organic connexion between people and State which underlies the latter notion imposes upon the conservative revolutionary as a necessary deduction that the forms of the State must adapt themselves to the internal and external transformation of the people, of the popular consciousness, of the popular degree of maturity. It also follows as a matter of principle that those forms of the State are 'good', i.e. suitable, which are favourable to the bodily and mental health and development of the organism that is the people; even as those forms of the State are 'bad', i.e. unsuitable, that are unfavourable and in-hibitive in these respects.

For the people is the content, the living, the organic; the State is the form, the dead, the organizational.

The experiences of recent years, and especially our experiences of the Hitler System, make it necessary to reject with the utmost possible emphasis the principle of the 'totalitarian State'.

The national idea, according to which man and his organic community the people should be the core of the social system, involves by its conservative nature the repudiation of any attempt to idolize an organizational form. No less decisively in favour of this repudiation is the recognition that the State, from its very nature, can only have regulative functions, that is to say can only influence and ought only to influence a part (though an important part) of the social life. Both the lower plane, that of the 'body' (= economic life), and still more the higher plane, that of the 'soul' (= culture), tend by their very nature to set themselves apart from the plane of the 'spirit' (= society), and claim for themselves independent fulfilment, unless the natural equilibrium is to be impaired, which will inevitably lead to the illness and ultimately to the death of the organism as a whole.

In accordance with the introductory thoughts to our Philosophical Foundations (see above, pp. 119 and foll.) the reader will, I think, understand these dissertations even if he finds I am making a somewhat unfamiliar use of terms. (This is mainly because the words—like old coins—have been worn thin by excessive use. They will need to be reminted in days to come.)

The lordly sense of superiority with which the genuine conservative always regards the State as nothing more than an instrument, a tool — as a 'suit of clothes' which fits the people more or less well — is justified, even as is justified the humble respect he has for the organism of the 'nation', in which he sees the durable whilst the State is the transient varying with the extant growth or ripeness of the nation.

## 2. THE FORM OF THE STATE

For these reasons, at bottom the State form is indifferent, and all we have to enquire is which form of State is most appropriate to the present ripeness (= age) and ideology of the German people.

For these reasons, more especially, the question monarchy or republic is of little moment. Our choice will be determined by our answer to the question, 'Which form of State will be most suitable to the German character and essential nature?' The more suitable the State is to the German character, the more harmonious will be its internal organization, and the more powerful will it be in a world where it is faced by other States.

The principle that only the best and most efficient among German men shall be summoned to lead the State, excludes hereditary monarchy, for it is contrary to probabilities that talent will be so perfectly transmitted by inheritance that the son of the best leader will also be the best leader of his people. An additional argument against hereditary monarchy is the principle that there must be no handicap in life, that there shall be equality of opportunity for all the citizens. A form of State in which a supreme position is assured, by the mere fact of birth, to the eldest son of the reigning monarch conflicts so drastically with the principle of equality of opportunity that it is self-condemned.

Remains to decide between an electoral monarchy and a republic. In either case the head of the State will be elected: in an electoral monarchy, for life; in a republic, for a specified term.

A short term certainly involves the danger that the president will be tempted, in order to favour his chances of re-election, to bribe the electors by concessions of one sort or another; and this will make dispassionate government unlikely. The danger of bias will be greater when the president is energetic and ambitious (two qualities that are otherwise desirable in a statesman), resulting in corruption when the electorate is small, in the courting of popularity when it is large.

Such dangers are obviated when the president (or monarch) is elected for life, for this makes him independent of the electors, and enables him to contemplate and carry out far-reaching schemes regardless of anything so mutable as popular favour.

For these reasons it seems to us that the best arrangement for Germany would be that the Reich should have a president elected for the term of his natural life. That would be conformable with the experience of more than a thousand years of German history, and it matters not whether the monarch so chosen is called an emperor or a president.

### 3. ADMINISTRATION

The president of the Reich, elected for life, will be the supreme representative of the State authority. The ministers appointed by and subordinate to him will merely be experts with advisory functions, and will not be responsible wielders of State power; they will be personally responsible to the president.

The second wielder of State authority will be the Great Council.

The Great Council will consist of the presidents of the provinces (from twelve to seventeen in number), the five ministers of State, and the presidium of the Reich Chamber of the Estates. It will therefore have about two dozen members, all of them persons of outstanding importance. By a simple majority vote, the Great Council will also elect the president of the Reich (who need not be a member of the Council).

The third wielder of State authority will be the Reich Chamber of Estates. This will consist of 110 members, 100 being elected and 10 being nominated. It stands at the head of the entire Estates System. (Fuller details will be found in Section Five, below.)

The three wielders of State authority will have equal powers. A law will require the assent of any two of them for enactment or repeal.

Stability in the management of the State will be ensured by the fact that the president of the Reich is elected for life, that he will command a majority in the Great Council (since he appoints the presidents of the provinces), and because, nominating ten members of the Reich Chamber of Estates, he will also have predominant influence in that body.

The position of the president of the Reich, which was outlined by the author in 1931, obtruded itself into the Hitler System after Hindenburg's death — but with the difference typical of the transitional character of the Hitlerian epoch, that here it was an inevitable outcome of circumstances, not the fruit of creative will. This accounts for the absurdity that the ministry de jure of the Reich still has in the main (as the Weimar constitution foresaw) de facto the character of a mere body of experts with advisory functions, and lacking the powers of responsible government.

But precisely because the president of the Reich will thus have a great deal of power, it is vital that there should be the two other wielders of State authority, to establish the eminently desirable modern form of 'authoritarian democracy', which is fundamentally distinct both from the dictatorship (of an individual or of a party) and from the mass dominion (of parties or councils). — Once more, fuller details will be found below in Section Five.

Here it becomes necessary to say something very important about the officialdom. In conformity with the essential nature of the genuine 'people's State' which we desire to establish, there must be no privileged officials. Probably there is no popular sentiment more widely diffused, and certainly there can be none better justified, than discontent with an officialdom which considers itself entitled to lead a sheltered life apart from the economic struggles of the broad masses of the people. Less than ever today do any exceptional achievements of the officialdom warrant such a position.

When as a matter of principle the 'official' has become nothing more than a 'public servant', he will have to fulfil all the demands for efficiency and hard work that are made of the members of the liberal professions, and to share in the vicissitudes of the general welfare. In other words, whereas in contemporary Germany the officials have peculiar rights in that they cannot be dismissed and are entitled to pensions — when the new order has been established, absolute security against dismissal will have been forfeited by officials of all grades, whilst the right to a pension will belong to every German citizen without exception.

It will be a firm principle with German socialism that a privileged and powerful officialdom — bureaucracy, in short — will be a deadly peril, against which the only safeguards are a maximum of self-government, and a minimum of official rights. That is why strict supervision and control of all public functionaries will be so imperative.

## 4. PROVINCIAL SUBDIVISION

One of the most difficult questions of German home policy, hitherto, has been the puerile one, unitarism or federalism? The question is of typically liberal origin, and it need hardly be said that the liberal answer has always been 'unitarism'.

Though a conservative German will no less certainly answer 'federalism', it must not be supposed that he dreams of making the present German States the units of this new federalism. These States nowise correspond to the organic integrality of the populations living within their 'borders'. They came into being as a result of the local dynasts' endeavour to bring as much territory and as many 'subjects' as possible under their respective sways — an endeavour which was most powerful (and also most deleterious to Germany) in the Habsburg monarchy.

It will, therefore, obviously be needful for Germany, as a start, to break up and rearrange these separate States.

I know that, as things are now, both Old Prussia and New Prussia will strongly oppose the disintegration of the State that passes by the name of Prussia, on the ground that it would be disastrous to the Reich because it would impair the formative energy of the Prussian spirit.

I have, indeed, too much respect for the Prussian spirit, and am too keenly aware of the important part it has played in German history, to be moved by any anti-Prussian resentment such as I might be supposed to have imbibed in my Bavarian homeland.

But my knowledge of the German character and of German history have convinced me that the Prussian particularist solution was no more than an arbitrary expedient — which did not cease to be an arbitrary expedient because it was advocated and adopted by Frederick the Great and then by Bismarck. My general understanding of historical interlacements convinces me, indeed, that in the epoch of the (liberal) national State there was no other way by which the Reich could be established than by the hegemony of Prussia. But the same understanding now informs me that the time is ripe for a revival of the old (conservative) idea of the Reich, an idea whose mystical interconnexion with the rebirth of the West is overwhelmingly confirmed by the history of the last thousand years.

The development of the German people into a true

German nation (which I regard as the substantial meaning of the German Revolution, demands and compels that Prussian particularism in all its forms shall be thrown into the melting-pot, demands and compels a wedding of the Frederician German type with the Theresian German type to procreate (anew) the true German — for to the true German appertains a European sense, which was so conspicuously and fatefully lacking in Prussian particularism.

This recognition of the necessarily unified character of the German State is not an acceptance of the ideal of liberal unitarism. For this unified German State must not be ruled centrally from one spot. There are such marked geopolitical, religious, and cultural differences within the German people as to forbid a uniformity that would conflict with the very nature of the Germans. Though, therefore, the coming German realm will be unified, it will be federally subdivided into provinces. The extant arbitrarily formed States and territories having been broken up, they will be rearranged into from twelve to fifteen provinces, each corresponding to a geopolitical, cultural, and tribal entity.

The weekly periodical I used to edit under the title of 'Der schwarze Front'[1] contains, in its issue of September 30, 1931, a sketch of the proposed provincial subdivision of the German Reich as it then existed, to which I refer readers who want more details.

The province will be subdivided into circles (Kreise), each having approximately the size of the present circles (in Bavaria, Bezirk; in Saxony, Amtshauptmannschaft;

---

[1] It has now [1936] become *Die deutsche Revolution*, Verlag Heinrich Grunov, Prague.

in Würtemberg, Oberamt; in Baden, Amtsbezirk; in Mecklenburg and Oldenburg, Amt).

Reich — province — circle will thus be the organizational subdivision of the administrative areas of the German State.

Each province will have its own president, who will hold office for seven years. He will be appointed by the president of the Reich, but the appointment will be subject to the approval of the Provincial Chamber of Estates. If this approval is withheld for two years in succession, the provincial president will have to retire, and the president of the Reich must appoint another.

In like manner the circle president will be appointed for five years by the provincial president, and his appointment will need the approval of the Circle Chamber of Estates. Here also, if approval is withheld once, the question will come up again after a year's interval.

The need for confirmation of the appointment of the chief provincial and circle officials by the respective Chambers of Estates implies the exercise of an extremely important influence by the popular assemblies. Thereby the presidents of circles and provinces will become at least as dependent upon the good will of the people as upon that of their official superiors, and this is all the more important because thus the popular influence in the Great Council will go far beyond that in any case exercised through the representatives directly elected by the people (the five chairmen of the Reich Chambers of Estates).

The prescription of a one-year-interval before a second vote by which the president of a province or a circle can be definitively dismissed safeguards these officials against excessive mutability of public opinion, and ensures in any case the continuous functioning of State authority.

## 5. THE ESTATES SYSTEM

### A. Abolition of the Party System

The most important inference from the conservative view that human beings (even the members of the same people) are unequal in bodily, mental, and religious respects, and therefore unequal in what they can do for the community, is the repudiation of the (pseudo-) democratic principle of equality.

A further inference is the recognition that every human being can only form valid judgments about things and persons that he knows from his own achievements and from personal experience. This involves the repudiation of the politico-parliamentary electoral system.

It is time to unveil the repulsive and gain-seeking falsehood of popular government which is an essential constituent of liberalism, which is disseminated by selfish groups of capitalists, promulgated by internationals of all kinds, maintained by demagogy that tickles the vanity of the masses and contributes to securing for various obscure forces an influence and leadership that would be impossible in a better-managed State.

That is why the German socialists unconditionally reject any kind of political election, any election by political parties and groups which always remain anonymous, and, conversely, why they insist that it is necessary to establish a system of popular representation by vocational estates.

On principle these demands signify the end of all political parties, and whatever kind of parliaments they may have formed. From their very nature political parties have a vital interest in sundering the people into factions, for they exist through producing such a cleavage, and their main task is to foster and intensify oppositions of every kind by means of the press, public meetings, etc. A genuine commonwealth of the people can, therefore, only be established by the destruction of the existing party system.

If I here reproduce without change what appears concerning this matter in the first edition (1931) of the *Aufbau des deutschen Sozialismus*, it is only to show in how inadequate, half-hearted, and therefore inveracious a way the Hitler System fulfilled this primary demand of the German Revolution. The necessary and eminently desirable dissolution of political parties was stayed as regards the dissolution of the Hitlerian Party; the (evil and corrupt) system of rule by political parties was replaced by the (still more evil and still more corrupt) system of rule by a monopolist party.

All complaints made of the party system apply with redoubled force to the monopolist party system of the Hitler regime, which has all the drawbacks of the multiple-party system and none of its advantages.

In my view the parliamentary form of party government is incomparably preferable to any kind of uncontrolled personal or party dictatorship — not forgetting that there are varieties of parliamentary party government, ranging from the ideal-democratic system of the

Swiss canton of Appenzell by way of the conservative-democratic system of Great Britain to the demagogic-democratic system of the Weimar Republic.

The fact that there are such diversities within the field of parliamentary democracy shows that where there are different preliminaries, at varying times and under various developmental conditions, there may be distinctive forms of democracy, and that it is consequently incumbent upon us to study what new kinds of democracy may be called for by existing circumstances.

Nor must we forget the signal fact that during the last decades of western social evolution there has been going on everywhere a 'massing' of the people which cannot fail to have momentous consequences. Owing to the rapid growth of towns, of enormous towns, tentacular towns, people have been uprooted from the countryside and 'intellectualized' in a way that has weakened their healthy instincts; this has been accompanied by a growing inclination to overrate both machinery and sport, these in their turn tending to hasten the general despiritualization of life. The net upshot has been the fateful change of the peoples into mere masses, a change which has increasingly affected all the European nations. Elsewhere,[1] discussing the matter in detail, I have given concrete instances of this trend and its effect upon political life. Here, then, it will suffice to reiterate my conclusion that this disastrous change from people to mass will necessarily involve the decay of all the old forms of democracy — a decay that is so con-

---

[1] See my book *Die deutsche Bartholomäusnacht* [the German Massacre of St Bartholomew], Reso-Verlag, Zurich, 1935, pp 129 and foll.

spicuously displayed by the cheapjack methods of the mass political parties of today.

A logical inference from this, reinforced by a knowledge of what has been happening in Germany, is that the revival of the old parties has become impossible.

The German people's passive acceptance of these (still no more than half-finished) workings of the Hitler System shows very clearly [in 1936] how accurate was the diagnosis of the situation I made five years ago, and how in this respect the Hitler System has been fulfilling the will of the German Revolution.

### B. Vocational Councils

It is of the utmost importance, therefore, to establish a new form of democracy which shall avoid the defects of the old kinds, shall make due allowance for the 'massing' which has occurred, shall go out to meet the dangers that have resulted therefrom, and shall overcome them within its own structure — trying, at the same time, to arrest, and as far as may be to reverse, this process of disintegration.

These things will only be possible if we can liberate once more the mighty energies of self-government, loosen the framework of society, educate the people by systematically encouraging political responsibility in the very lowest strata of the community, and thus consolidate a supporting tier, without which authoritative democracy is impossible.

We must therefore create, instead of the bureaucratically dictatorial State of fascist, bolshevist, or parliamentary irresponsibility, the genuinely popular State of German democracy and aristocratic responsibility.

The principles and forms of an aristocratically responsible way of carrying on the State have been expounded in the first four sections of this chapter. We now have to consider the principles and forms of supervision and collaboration by the people, of self-government by the estates, of what I call 'German democracy'.

Starting from the conservative view enunciated above (p. 189) that a human being can only form valid judgments about things and persons that he knows from his own achievements and from personal experience, we arrive at the vocation as the basis of every 'choice', every election, that the individual German can make in his own sphere of achievement and personal experience.

Therewith is fulfilled another vital demand based upon the conservative view, that only those citizens shall have seat and vote in the Thing who contribute a prescribed minimum by way of achievement on behalf of the community, in a word, only those who work.

The demand that the electors should be personally known is fulfilled by the circumstance that the 'constituency' shall be the smallest 'administrative unit' — the circle.

The German citizen will therefore make one primary electoral act, within his own vocation and his own circle.

In each circle there will be elected five vocational chambers, or vocational councils, namely:

> the Workers' Council of the Circle,
> the Peasants' Council of the Circle,
> the Council of the Liberal Professions,
> the Council for Industry and Trade,
> the Council for Employees and Officials.

Each vocational council of the circle will consist of twenty-five members elected for three years.

These vocational councils will be the only popular assemblies that are the outcome of general, equal, secret, and direct election by persons active in a vocation or retired therefrom.

They are exclusively vocational representations of persons united by common interests.

This fact prescribes their sphere of activity. The vocational councils will deal with all vocational interests; will supervise wages, working conditions, vocational training, etc.; they will be the experts to be consulted upon all vocational questions by the national administration; and, above all, they will decide matters of fiefs and 'entails'. They alone will nominate the candidate for any fief that becomes vacant, and the State will ratify the appointment through the instrumentality of the appropriate circle-president — or else will refuse to ratify it, in which case the vocational council concerned will have to make a fresh nomination.

The vocational electors will naturally do their utmost to elect as members of the vocational council the persons best fitted for their task, being guided by a knowledge of the candidates both in vocational and in private life.

The further development of the vocational councils will accord with the structure of the administration in this way, that the vocational councils of the circles will elect the five vocational councils of the province, consisting of fifty members each, belonging to the appropriate vocation; and the vocational councils of the provinces will elect the five vocational councils of the Reich, each consisting of one hundred members, belonging to the appropriate vocation.

The decisive feature here is that these elections of the provincial chambers and the Reich chambers is not primary, but indirect; not by the ultimate electors, but by the members of the next lower grade of vocational representation. The object here is, of course, to ensure that the most capable and effective vocational representatives shall rise into the higher bodies, which will be guaranteed all the more securely by indirect election without any canvassing of the primary electorate because the election of the fittest is in the interest of each vocation.

The members of the provincial vocational council will be elected for five years, those of the Reich vocational council for seven.

The sphere of activity of the higher councils will be identical with that of the circle councils. Substitutes will have to be elected to a lower council in place of those appointed to a higher council.

Thus the vocational councils will represent the interests of all the active workers in Germany.

It is important to note that the self-government of these councils will be absolutely independent, whereas in Italy and Russia the State and the respective monopolist parties dominate (that is to say interfere with) the self-government of the active workers. This is especially marked in Italy, where none but members of the Fascist Party or the fascist unions are eligible for election and entitled to vote, the representation of the active workers being thus limited to a small fraction of the population (carefully sifted by the organs of the State), consisting of persons in relation to whom the masses of active workers have no rights whatever. (It is the same here in Germany under the Hitler System, without even the trifling fragment of the corporations.)

It is somewhat different in Russia, where (in theory, at least) the whole mass of active workers has the suffrage. Still, the different categories of active workers have different voting powers, and some are expressly disfranchized. Five peasant votes correspond to one worker vote — though we are told that there is to be a change in the next elections; and many persons engaged in 'bourgeois' vocations, notably the intellectual professions, are disfranchized. It is significant that in Russia the motions that are to be voted on are decided by the party, and merely have to be 'approved' by the assemblies. Also we note in Russia a very remarkable fact that whereas in the councils of the lower grade there are many non-party members (of course persons acceptable to the party), there is a much larger proportion of communists in the middle-grade bodies, and the highest councils consist exclusively of party members. This signifies that there can be no genuine, independent, democratic representation of the interests of all active workers.

Contrariwise the war-cry of German socialism is that we shall ensure unrestricted, truly democratic self-government by all the active workers of the population. There must be no influence exerted by, no dependence upon, any powerful group or party, and least of all upon the State. No matter what the State may desire, under the German system any German who enjoys the confidence of others that pursue the same vocation will be able to make his way into the highest offices by which the State is controlled and led; even becoming a member of the Reich Chamber of Estates or the Great Council. This will mean the most complete democracy attainable and without a chance of its degenerating into demagogic rule.

### C. Chambers of Estates

Inasmuch as the vocational councils of the circle, the province, and the Reich will represent nothing but vocational interests, they must be supplemented by general popular representation.

In each administrative unit (circle, province, Reich) there will, consequently, be formed out of its vocational councils a Chamber of Estates, as follows.

The Circle Chamber of Estates will consist of twenty-five persons elected by the vocational councils of that circle and three additional members nominated by the circle president. These nominees must be eminent and respected inhabitants of the circle.

The Provincial Chamber of Estates will consist of fifty persons elected by the vocational councils of the province and five additional members nominated by the president of the province.

The Reich Chamber of Estates will consist of one hundred persons elected by the vocational councils of the Reich and ten additional members nominated by the president of the Reich.

Of decisive importance to the composition of the Chambers of Estates is it to make sure that they shall faithfully reflect the sociological stratification of the circle, the province, or the Reich. For this reason the

197

various vocational councils will not elect the same number of members each to the appropriate Chamber of Estates, but a number proportional to the composition of the population in the administrative area concerned. If, for instance, in a province there are 40% of workers, 25% of peasants, 10% of tradespeople, 10% practising the liberal professions, and 15% of employees or officials, then the membership of the Chamber of Estates must comprise the same respective proportions. Of the fifty members of this provincial Chamber of Estates, twenty would be industrial workers; twelve, peasants; five, tradesmen; five, members of the liberal professions; eight, employees or officials. One necessary limitation to this would be that no vocation must have more than 50% of the members of the Chamber, so that it would not be possible for one of the estates to command a clear majority over the others.

In each administrative area the presidium of a Chamber of Estates would be formed by the five chairmen of the vocational councils.

The sphere of activity of a Chamber of Estates is fundamentally different from that of a vocational council.

The Chambers of Estates form an important part of the State administration and State leadership.

Their collaboration in every governmental measure is direct insofar as every decree by a circle president or provincial president would need the approval of the appropriate Chamber of Estates. Moreover, as explained in Section Four of this chapter (pp. 188 and 189), the circle president and the provincial president will need to enjoy the confidence of their respective Chambers of

Estates for the proper performance of their official duties.

But the right of veto possessed by a Circle Chamber of Estates or a Provincial Chamber of Estates only becomes effective when exerted, about the same matter, for a second time after a year's interval. This measure cuts both ways: for, on the one hand, it prevents the holding-up of measures urgently required for the good of the State; and, on the other hand, the permanent enforcement of an unpopular measure, or the continuance in office of an unpopular president, will be prevented by the system of popular representation.

In addition the activity of the Chambers of Estates will render possible their authoritative supervision of the whole State administration in the area under their control, and especially their collaboration in matters of consumption, prices, quality, etc.

The duration of the Chambers of Estates, in conformity with that of the vocational councils, will be three years for the circle, five for the province, seven for the Reich.

The special duties of the Reich Chamber of Estates as the legislative body, and the further duties of its presidium of five (consisting of the chairmen of the five Reich vocational councils) has been discussed in Section Three of this chapter.

Not unimportant is it to mention that representative services in the vocational councils and Chambers of Estates will be honorary. Compensation will be allowed for loss of time and out-of-pocket expenses, but there will be no financial advantage in holding such a post.

The decisive importance of this scheme for the representation of the estates, lies in the fact that thereby the popular will can find expression throughout the work of administration no matter what the State authorities may do or desire to do.

The distinction between vocational councils and Chambers of Estates, both as regards their composition and as regards their duties, is of the utmost moment.

Whilst the vocational councils give expression and influence to the vertical stratification of the German people, the Chambers of Estates represent the horizontal stratification, and thus give a cross-section through the interests of various parts of the population in all areas of the Reich.

The councils represent purely vocational interests, so that their duties are correspondingly restricted to the particular vocations and the relation of these to the State; but the Chambers secure for the localities a general popular representation, and consequently form an important part of the general State administration and State guidance.

Of especial consequence is it that thereby will be ensured a direct and lasting popular control of the State and its officials in all parts of the State apparatus.

In the fascist State there is no such control; in the bolshevik State it can only be exercised 'by way of the Party' (which is almost identical with the State); and in the parliamentary State, at the best, control can only be exercised by unseating the government, which is often a difficult matter. But the Circle and Provincial Chambers of Estates, with their right of veto over circle president and territorial president, can control the State apparatus permanently, directly, and effectively; can control it from the bottom to the top through the instrumentality of independent popular representatives. Hereby we realize the idea of a people's State as contrasted with bureaucracy.

# CHAPTER FOUR

# CULTURAL POLICY OF GERMAN SOCIALISM

## I . CONSERVATIVE REALISM

IN conformity with our knowledge of the completeness of the revolution that is inevitable, and is therefore in progress, we realize that there is also going on a revolutionary change in peoples' minds. They are forming a new estimate of the meaning of life and of the task that awaits mankind.

The philosophy of the liberal epoch has been and still is materialism. Nothing typifies Marxism more plainly than the fact that it is tainted with alien views of socialism, that its program is shaped by the materialist philosophy which it shares with liberalism.

Before the French Revolution we already encounter traces of a new outlook on life — the outlook of those who aspire to break away from their allegiance to God, and to take their stand exclusively upon the logical plane of a human knowledge that has been freed from sparks of the divine.

This rationalist way of looking at things involved a number of serious errors. The rationalists and materialists believed themselves able to explain nature; but they failed to grasp nature in its entirety, in its relations to life; they recognized no other phenomena than those that could be numbered, weighed, and measured, and thus subjected to what they regarded as 'law'. All that lay beyond this, which was non-rational and therefore 'unreasonable', all that was inaccessible to the reason, to the understanding, having been deliberately excluded from observation, they then went on trying to force their rationalist laws upon the non-rational.

The development of science, which convinced them they would be able to understand and explain everything, induced an overweening pride which made them regard the understanding of the ego as the measure of all things, and recognize as real only that which the understanding (thus limited) could grasp. Matter and force were the foundations of all being. The rationalists, the materialists, felt that they could really understand matter, but force remained inexplicable. Still, this did not bother these would-be 'explainers'. The contemplation of dead matter, of its atomic structure, of the juxtaposition of these atoms and their mechanical relations in a universe where they were moved by named but inexplicable forces, became the foundation of their picture of the world, the basis of the materialist outlook — of materialism.

To us conservatives this attempt of the liberals to evade the mysteries of life, the subordinations to destiny, with the methods of a soulless logic, seems to us as childish as would be the endeavour to ascertain the perfume of a flower with a yardstick or a weighing machine. Humbly and modestly we recognize that the decrees of fate lie outside human control, and that it behoves man to abide by these decrees — in a word, to accept 'God's will'. We know and accept His will as the presupposition of all that befalls man and of all human action, and we solve the eternal enigma of the freedom of the human will by saying that the 'What' lies without the sphere of that will, but the 'How' within.

We thus find a new significance for life in the fulfilment of the 'God-willed' specific peculiarities of our people, in the affirmation and perfectionment of the people's soul as a revelation from God.

But we should only be making a blunder akin to that of the materialists were we, in our turn, to proclaim idealism as an exclusive philosophy of the world.

Indubitably it has been one of the great and never-to-be-forgotten services of liberalism in general and of Marxism in particular to have proved how valuable and important to life are material forces, material relations, and material functions; a service which abides, however much the liberals and the Marxians may have underestimated the value and importance of ideal forces, ideal relations, and ideal functions.

Were the German socialists, instead, to overestimate the value and importance of idealism, they would be false to the crucial doctrine of the neo-conservative organic philosophy, according to which the true and all-embracing reality of life is discoverable in the relations and the functions of the necessarily unified forces of body, mind, and soul. We are justified therefore in speaking of conservative realism as the typical philosophy of the German socialists.

## 2. RELIGION AND CHURCH

Conservative realism not only regards the power of faith as one of the most splendid manifestations of the soul, but also affirms the greatness and everlastingness of the religious sentiment which unites the human soul with God.

But our humility towards every true religion must not blind us to the fact that not only religious ideas, but also (and even more) religious forms, i.e. the Churches, are intertwined with the specific peculiarities of the various nations and with the general laws of human transitoriness which finds expression in the mutability of all the phenomena of life.

Here, then, arises (more especially in view of the turn the German Revolution has taken of late), the question where Christianity stands in the picture.

We should be false to the teachings of history were we to deny that the source of Christianity did not flow from the spot where the heart of the West beats. But if, as we showed in the chapter on Philosophical Foundations, the concept 'West' includes the religious elements of history as well as the racial and geopolitical ones, it follows undeniably that the mighty experience of Christianity has been an inseparable constituent of the West, and that any attempt to eliminate it would be as foolish and impracticable as to attempt to make the impressions of two thousand years of history non-existent.

This does not mean that the mutations of the West, as determined by the eternal law of growing older and by the rhythmic change in ideas, will not have a decisive influence upon Christianity itself. If today far-seeing Christian theologians speak and write both of the 'Germanization of Catholicism' and of the 'Catholicization of Protestantism',[1] this shows to how great an extent muta-

---

[1] Cf. the article entitled 'Katholische Kirche und National-Sozialismus' in the *Neue Zürcher Zeitung*, No. 1268, July 21, 1935

tion is going on in Christianity. A glance at the religious and organizational struggles in the Protestant Churches and in the Greek Orthodox Church, at the changed and changing relations between Catholicism and Protestantism, and also between the Catholic Church and the Greek Orthodox Church, will confirm the view that political and economic structural changes in the West are bound to have a decisive influence upon its religious and cultural forms.

All this indicates that Christianity and Europe are not antitheses, but that, on the contrary, the mental attitude of the West has been formed and determined by Christianity — which itself, though beginning outside Europe, has largely been domiciled there for ages.

In this connexion the reader will do well to refer back to the last paragraph on p. 98, where I deal with the question of the relation of the Eastern Catholic (Orthodox) Churches to Western Europe.

The author does not wish, nor does he feel competent, to go more deeply into these eminently personal religious problems. Enough to have referred to the matter in general terms, and to have recognized (with considerable gratification) that inside and outside Christianity great and vigorous movements are heralding a religious renaissance, though without as yet having any obvious effect upon the extant Churches.

Above all he is interested in the relations between State and Church, and is strongly in favour of the separation of the two.

This separation would mean the end of an unworthy dependence of the Church upon the State, and also the beginning of a free development of the extant Churches.

It would still be the obvious duty of the State to protect the Churches against attack from without.

A separation of the main Church in a country from the State would likewise be beneficial to other religious communities, and would favour the growth of all genuine religious movements, with whose internal affairs the State should never interfere.

The proclamation of the freedom of faith and conscience would be usefully supplemented by a recognition of the freedom of art and science, whose healthy growth needs independence from the rule of the average man — and what more can any State be in these respects? Then only will the intellectual and artistic rivalry of the European nations, an Olympiad of the spirit, be really fruitful, so that a cultural renovation of Europe will be no less certain than a political and economic revival.

The press requires special consideration. Though on principle we demand the freedom of the press, liberty does not mean libertinage, as it has done often enough under liberal auspices. Guarantees will have to be given to ensure that freedom shall not be misused.

The most effective guarantee will be insistence that every contribution to a periodical shall be signed. The abolition of anonymity and of the editorial 'we' will make the writer responsible both politically and legally. Another valuable safeguard will be that a sharp distinction shall be drawn between politics and business. It must be made impossible for the advertisement columns to influence the 'news'. This will be achieved by an advertisement monopoly, and the consequently reduced cost of production and distribution in the case of many commodities will have a good effect on prices.

### 3 . THE NEW SCHOOL

The position and form of the school is of direct interest to the present work.

The position and form of the school are dependent upon the importance attached to the school, and upon the tasks assigned to it by popular culture and the German State.

For the State, the school is the principal means by which the intellectual leaders are sifted out. Though earlier I have castigated and repudiated the liberal illusion concerning human equality, I nevertheless ardently champion the conservative doctrine that equality of opportunity is essential — that, as far as can be, all should be given an equal start in the race of life. There must be no needless handicaps.

Nothing but an equal start for all citizens can ensure that there shall be an organic stratification into 'estates', that is to say into groups of similar, equally competent, equally directed human beings whose occupation is in harmony with their 'calling' — instead of a disastrous stratification into 'classes', this meaning into groups of dissimilar, variously competent, variously directed human beings who follow the same occupation, not because they have a 'calling', but because they have been forced to.

To give an equal start, education at all the schools must be free, and the pupils will be gratuitously supplied with the requisite books and materials. Arrangements must also be made to render it possible for every pupil at an elementary school to pass on to a higher school, no matter where he lives — for of course there will not be a secondary school in every district. The cost of attending such schools at a distance from the pupils' homes will be defrayed by the State.

A people's community can have only one kind of primary schools, at which there will be separate classes for more highly gifted and less highly gifted children. When the course at the elementary school is finished, education will be continued at a technical or vocational school, in other cases at a higher school, and later, in suitable cases, at a university. The uniformity of system does not mean that all the schools will be exactly alike, for they will be variously adapted to peculiarities in the provinces and circles.

The subjects taught in the elementary school will be German, history, arithmetic, knowledge of the homeland, the beginnings of natural science, bodily exercises, gardening, simple technical training — the aim being, not to 'impart information' but to educate Germans. The age for attendance at the elementary school will be from six to fourteen, inasmuch as not until after puberty will the vocation be chosen and vocational training begin. Before that, the child will be growing up into the German cultural world, without having his mind unduly diverted towards alien cultures during the receptive years of childhood.

At puberty a child will pass on from the elementary school, either to a vocational (technical) school, or else to a higher school where training in the direction of the intellectual professions will be carried on.

At a high school, education will be more diversified. Since German culture will have been thoroughly instilled at the elementary school, alien cultures can now be taught, for there will be little risk of alien contamination.

When the high-school education is finished, selection of pupils for the university will take place. Here it is not simply the 'amount of knowledge' that has been acquired which will be taken into consideration, but also the character that will be considered desirable in a person destined to be one of the future leaders of the German people.

The decisive feature of the selection will be, not that the youngsters (or their parents for them) want university education, but the will of the community, as expressed through the teaching staffs and the examiners (who must have had plenty of practical experience). Mistakes can be avoided by insisting, not only on promotion certificates from the school which is being left, but on the passing of an entrance examination at the higher school or university to which the pupil is going.

These methods will fulfil the aims of any careful and intelligent system of State leadership, that the best elements of the whole population shall be given a good chance of rising to the top. Only a lasting and self-regulative process of renovation can prevent the occurrence of 'morbid stasis' here and there in the national organism.

It is expedient to point out that for such a structural alteration in the German educational system, a spiritual change throughout will be indispensable.

Hitherto the main object of schooling has been to 'impart information', but henceforward it will be regarded as at least equally important to train character. As a result, not only will the pupil's character have a decisive influence upon his chances of promotion to a higher school or a university, but the educational institutions will thereby be profoundly modified both subjectively and objectively.

More especially the universities will differ greatly from our present ones. They will lose the duplex character they now have of being institutions both for teaching and for research. Whereas, nowadays, for practical reasons more emphasis is usually laid upon research than upon teaching, in days to come there will be great stress on teaching and on character-training. The universities will be of a collegiate type, that is to say they will be circumscribed institutions, in the country rather than in towns, with an attached economic branch where in the vacations the students will be engaged in practical labours. The two first terms will be devoted to general philosophical, historical, and artistic studies, after which the separation into faculties will begin. Great value will be attached to sports, comradeship, and the like: each university will probably have its own tradition, to the maintenance of which sometime-students' clubs will contribute.

The higher schools will be analogous to our present gymnasia, but early specialization will be avoided. Special importance will be attached to high schools having courses conducted in foreign tongues, which will not only promote close touch with the intellectual world of foreign nations, but will encourage the appearance of many good linguists among the Germans. (This will further have a good effect upon the national minorities living in Germany, and will encourage foreigners to come to German schools.)

One may hope that former pupils of a high school will continue to take a lively interest in its work, partly in the indirect form of patronage, partly in the direct form of assistance as examiners. These outsiders, both in the high school and in the elementary school, will assist the teaching staff in deciding a pupil's chances of promotion.

It is of fundamental importance that by thus regulating promotion the State should be able to prevent the overstocking of the country's professional intelligentsia, for any such overproduction of intellectuals or would-be intellectuals is most unwholesome to the social organism.

## 4. ARMY AND LABOUR SERVICES

However much we may insist on the need for a sifting by character, the school, from its very nature, will always tend to lay more weight upon intelligence tests.

How important it is therefore that schooling should be followed by another method of selection which allows adequately for the fact that in human beings the formation of character is not completed until after puberty, when the first educational period is over.

This supplementary testing will be effected in the universal labour service and in the voluntary army service.

For all young Germans of both sexes the close of early vocational training will be followed by a year of labour service in which the pupil will have to learn a handicraft. This year of labour service, during which the pupils will lead a comradely life that will be of considerable social importance, will also enable young Germans to revise their choice of a vocation, and will subject them to a process of selection that will help to disclose (after they have left the elementary school) those that are fitted for an intellectual vocation.

Of peculiar importance in selection by character will also be the period of voluntary military service for those that undertake it. This follows from the constitutional inequality of human beings, a recognition of which I have several times explained as one of the main features of the conservative philosophy.

Whereas a year of labour service will be compulsory, report for army service will be a voluntary affair. Inasmuch as military service will continue for several years, is not associated with the acquisition of new, privately useful knowledge, and involves considerable risk in the event of war, we may be sure that none but the nationally useful young fellows will wish to enter the army. In this way will be ensured the racial selection of those who will form the supporting stratum of the German socialist State.

The outstanding value of such a selection, which will confer on those who are sifted out a new title to nobility, will be that the title is acquired, not by birth, but by personal choice.

The extreme political importance of such a sustaining stratum, which will extend through all vocations and estates, can be underlined once more by providing that every person who occupies a highly esteemed un-remunerated position (all magistrates, guardians, trustees, etc.) shall be taken from this stratum.

## 5. GERMAN LAW, JUSTICE, AND RIGHT

Our account of the national culture would be inadequate should we fail to insist how essential it is that this culture shall favour the development of a German system of law, justice, and right.

It is self-evident from the national outlook that there can be no such thing as 'law per se', for the consciousness of right and the prevailing forms of law derive from the peculiarities of each people, from the age it has reached, and from the ideas that are at any time dominant.

That basic notion secured expression in our demand for a new economic law, and I have again and again stressed the national peculiarity of this economic law of German socialism.

But the law relating to persons needs a no less radical transformation than the law relating to things. It is preposterous to suppose that the present Civil Code can remain in force for as much as a day after the German Revolution has become effective.

Without going into too much detail I may mention as the fundamental idea of German law that the protection of honour is more important than the protection of things and rights. Another very important notion is that the Roman-Christian idea of punishment must be replaced by the Teutonic idea of reparation or compensation, and that the essential purpose of legal activity is not to discover individual blame, but to prevent injury to society.

The basic difference between the German law of to-morrow and the Civil Code of today will result in a complete change as regards punishments, and, above all, will reduce to a minimum the present absurd practice of punishing people by depriving them of liberty. As regards the enormous majority of offences, the cruel punishment of depriving the offender of liberty will give place to making him compensate whoever has been injured by imposing a fine which will be levied in case of need by making the offender work in a State workhouse without imprisonment. All offences against the community will be expiated by excluding the offender from the community temporarily or permanently, either by banishment or death. Thereby a repetition of the offence will be prevented.

Of decisive value for the carrying out of such ideas, especially during the period of transition, will be the abolition of expert courts in which judges and lawyers function. Instead there will be peoples' courts, where the sound instincts of the people can be trusted to observe the principles of German law, justice, and right until new legal forms have been elaborated.

## 6. ELITE AND IDEAL TYPE

The foregoing remarks upon the cultural program of German socialism are fragmentary and sketchy, this being partly due to the nature of the topic and partly to my own inadequacy. Still, I can supplement them by saying a few more words about their aim.

Their aim is to insist upon the need for cultivating an elite of the German people, in accordance with an ideal type that shall conform to the essential nature of the Germans.

This ideal type must be deeply rooted in the constitutional characteristics of the German people, and must therefore have the traits which the study of German history from its beginnings has made familiar to us; and yet, on the other hand, it must be modern enough to conform with the requirements of the socialist order to be established in the twentieth century.

Both demands will be fulfilled by producing the Old-

German type of knight, the chivalrous being whose best characteristics are embodied in all the greatest figures of German civilization, and who stand forth from the earlier (conservative) epochs of German history.

German education must be concentrated upon the production of this knightly, this chivalrous type, even as English education is concentrated upon the production of the type of the 'gentleman' which has been maintained for generations.

Here it becomes needful to return briefly to the problem of the upbuilding of the State. Before, when we were considering the revolutionary birth of the new order, we could only answer negatively the problem of how to produce this supporting stratum (by referring to the fact that the party system would have to be abolished); but now, again insisting upon the revolutionary genesis of the new order, we can throw light on the matter positively.

The production, the culture, of a supporting stratum, of an élite, is the vital problem of the new order, and upon its solution will depend the permanency and the satisfactory working of German socialism.

It will not suffice to do no more than formulate the principles of selection for intelligence and character, and to organize the process of selection by the schools, the labour service, and the voluntary army, for we shall also have to explain what will guide us in the actual practice of our methods of selection.

The picture of the new order proclaimed in this work, the new order of national freedom, social justice, and European collaboration, will be crowned by the declaration that the élite, the ideal type we aim at installing as leaders of Germany shall be the 'knights', that mighty creation which appeared so early in the West; which, unrestricted by national frontiers, became symbolic of the whole European community; and is now, consistently enough, being revived simultaneously with the resurrection of the West.

For this, and nothing else, is the meaning and the content of the German Revolution:

The Resurrection of the West.

# APPENDIXE

# PREFACE TO THE FIRST EDITION
## OF THE *AUFBAU*

THIS work is the first attempt at a complete transformation of German life in the sense of that mighty revolution which has been going on under our eyes since 1914. It is, in a sense, an account of the structure of the new crystal whose coming we foresee, whose forms we can deduce from the nature of the lye, from the forces that animate it, and the laws under which it works.

This remark exemplifies both the defects and the merits of such an attempt. The precise thinker would like to be shown finality, with every detail made manifest, and a timetable accurately drawn. But we are dealing with organic processes which defy accuracy of this sort. We recognize that organic processes are subject to their own internal laws, and it is from these that issue the forms which are predictable in accordance therewith. The better acquainted we are with these laws, the more fully will our predictions be confirmed by the reality. We conservative revolutionaries (for thus do I and my friends regard ourselves) are always aware that the organic process is primary, and that our schemata can be no more than sketches of what will go on within that process. In other words, when there is a conflict between life and a plan, life is always right, and the plan must be modified to suit it.

Despite these provisos and limitations, it seems expedient to draft our plan, for this will help to explain and give a meaning to what has been happening since 1914, and to all the sacrifices of wealth and blood that have been demanded of the German people during these eighteen years. It will console us, will encourage us to bear the last years of the transition, will give us strength to further the new developments; for awareness of what is happening, when it comes to countless Germans, will give them a sense of purpose which can accelerate the changes and make the sacrifices seem less onerous. The clearer the grasp of the direction and the better the preparations, the less resistance will there be, and the smaller the sacrifices.

It seems to us as if the tediousness of the process we term the German Revolution were an indication given by fate that the German people must systematically and deliberately prepare for the revolution, must recognize that the sacrifices of wealth and blood demanded are not more than the organism of the German people (no longer very young) can properly be expected to bear, and that the last violent act of birth can be achieved with a minimal loss of energy.

That is how the author and his friends contemplate the German situation, and they believe it to be incumbent on them to explain what they have learned from the last two decades of German history, to indicate the nature of the trend which discloses itself — and to show how its fulfilment offers the only way of restoring health to the German people. To promote such a restoration of health must assuredly be the aim of German policy.

Berlin.                                                                  Autumn, 1931.

# POSTFACE TO THE FIRST EDITION
## OF THE *AUFBAU*

WITHIN the narrow framework of a sketch of the upbuilding of German socialism I have tried to give an account of the new order whose establishment will supply a meaning to all the sacrifices of the last two decades. I know only too well that many important details have been omitted, but I trust that the intelligent reader will be able to fill in the gaps for himself.

There is one question I have intentionally refrained from trying to answer — how realization should be or can be secured. Even when the question has been mooted, it will be plain from the (repeatedly stressed) organic nature of the process that the answer cannot be a simple one.

Still, some parts of the answer are concrete enough. Necessarily the change will occur by way of revolution. All organic new-formation demands, in the last resort, a violent act — as is seen plainly enough in birth, though here the new-formation has been completed some time before. In our view, then, the violent act is not the beginning but the end of the revolution, the end of the reconstruction of the feelings, the thoughts, and the will of the Germans.

Another signpost on this road to the German Revolution is that a system can never be overthrown by the tools belonging to that system, but only by the tools that belong to the coming system, the one destined to be victorious. He, therefore, who uses liberal weapons to defeat a liberal system, will inevitably fail. Practical political consequences of this view are that we must ruthlessly oppose any democratic choice, any participation in a coalition with the old system, any opportunist attempt to maintain a portion of the system or one of its essential measures.

Of great importance, finally, is it to recognize that this revolution will not be made by the masses, but by a small number of persons who are ready to take risks, who have in their minds a clear picture of the new order, who are sufficiently self-sacrificing and sufficiently pugnacious to stake their lives in the hope of making their picture a reality.

This demands strength of character; readiness to endure solitude, persecution, mental and spiritual isolation. Unless the would-be revolutionist is prepared, as were Lenin and his associates, to risk exile or a long term in Siberia, fate will not hold him worthy to share responsibility for establishing the new order.

It is my daily prayer that great numbers of Germans see this and possess the required energy, so that at length there may be established in Germany the new order on behalf of which millions of the best of my fellow-countrymen have died.

Hail Germany!

# PREFACE TO THE SECOND EDITION
## OF THE *AUFBAU*

NEARLY five years have passed since the first edition of this book was published.

They have been eventful years: and Adolf Hitler's rise to power on January 30, 1933, substantially forms part of the contents of my book.

It is obvious that the second edition might pay heed to many other happenings which five years ago were not so manifest as was the likelihood of Hitler's rise. If, nevertheless, little change has been needed in the second edition, this shows the general accuracy of our view of the German Revolution, and amounts to a proof of the conformity of history to law — a notion that was embodied in our Philosophical Foundations.

The purpose of this book having been to draft the Structure of German Socialism, i.e. to give a design for the New Germany (as part of what will certainly be a New Europe), polemic was needless, just as little as an architect is disposed to argue about or find justifications for this or that detail of his drawings of a new cathedral (except where argument may be needed to clear up some otherwise doubtful point).

No, what was necessary, now and again, was to show that the draft paid due heed to extant data, and yet solved all the important problems that arose. Also it was important that the author should make his meaning clear, even as an architect must clearly show what he is planning to build. But the architect is not concerned with the question whether those who examine his plans will agree with him in every detail.

Of course such a method of demonstration involves a certain coldness, a lack of impetus, a dryness of exposition. But one

P

who, beyond the details, can see the great aim, one who bears within his own mind a vision of the cathedral of German socialism, one who feels the rhythm of life that pulsates beneath the abundance of social and economic details — such a one will grasp the essential spirituality of a dry architectural design, and will gain thereby the will-to-action without which knowledge and experience are no better than a tale told by an idiot, full of sound and fury, signifying nothing.

It is the will-to-action that transforms such a design as this from 'words, words, words' into a play of motive forces, and sounds a fanfare that induces all those who wish to mould the future to get together and start building the cathedral, New Germany, New Europe.

Prague.                                                Spring, 1936.

# POSTFACE TO THE SECOND EDITION
## OF THE *AUFBAU*

THE postface to the second edition of this book cannot content itself with generalities like those of the postface to the first edition, but must start from the fact of the Hitler System, and show the downfall of that system to be an indispensable preliminary to German socialism.

There has been no change in my general attitude to the Hitler System and to the party which sustains it. As I explained in my book *Die deutsche Bartholomäusnacht* [the German Massacre of St. Bartholomew, Reso-Verlag, Zurich, 1935], the Hitler System represents the (transient) Gironde epoch of the German Revolution, the interlude of revolutionary feelings and reactionary forms, which arises spontaneously out of a progressive internal radicalization, and thereby (mostly by a detour into war) clears the ground for an epoch of revolutionary construction.

This observation supplies the task, the strategy, and the tactics of the German socialists as against the Hitler System. With uncompromising energy and with any and every means (other than those which might run counter to their own ideas), and with unswerving resolution, they must work for the overthrow of the Hitler System.

The decisive point is that this struggle can only be successful if, and in so far as, they have recognized and solved the urgent economic, social, and cultural problems. Hitler was only possible and inevitable because these urgent problems had not been solved — and Hitler will fall because he, too, has not solved them.

# APPENDIXES

It behoves us to effect the overthrow of the Hitler System; it behoves us, therefore, above all, to solve these urgent problems, and thus to inaugurate a new epoch of German and European history, whose business it is to give human life once more a meaning and a goal.

# DANGER OF THE PARTITION OF GERMANY

[Translation of the first January issue in 1937 of 'Die deutsche Revolution', a bi-monthly issued as the organ of the Black Front, edited by Otto Strasser, published (then) in Prague and Copenhagen.]

## DANGER OF THE PARTITION OF GERMANY

THE Hitler System will bring war, and war will bring the partition of Germany, unless a Socialist Revolution in Germany comes in time to prevent it.

With deep concern all patriotic Germans watch the opening of 1937, for their observations convince them that this will be a crucial year.

The Hitler System is, with inevitable consistency, being driven towards the end, along the road it entered on June 30, 1934 [the date of the Blood Bath].

Before this, Hitler had not yet made his choice between the two alternatives that were open to him at the beginning of that year — Socialist Revolution and Fascist War — which from the first were implicit in the nature, the theory, and the practice of the Hitler System.

On June 30, 1934, this system entered the bloody road leading to war, for by the murder of the advocates of the second revolution Adolf Hitler blocked the path that would have led to German socialism. The question whether in this matter he was driver or driven is of little consequence to our political judgment.

Since then, with somnambulist confidence, he has been

advancing towards war, whose successive stages — armament, compulsory military service, the fortification of Rhineland, Danzig, two years' army service, the treaty between Germany and Japan — are still fresh in all men's memories.

However just and necessary it was and is, for the sake of our national freedom and the future of Germany, to shake off the fetters of the Treaty of Versailles, it was and is no less unreasonable and criminal to adopt and advocate German imperialism in place of the imperialism of those who coerced us in 1919.

Apart from the fact that one injustice is not overcome by substituting for it another injustice, every glance at German and European history shows that a forcible dictatorship will neither bring freedom and safety to our own nation, nor peace and unity to Europe.

The freedom and safety of Germany, the peace and unity of Europe are not attainable by means of the old methods of brute force, but only by means of the ideas of a new order.

The ideas that will bring about the new order that is vital to a better future and essential to our very lives are the ideas of the German Revolution, the ideas of:

> National Freedom,
> Social Justice,
> European Collaboration.

The Hitler System's betrayal of the German Revolution is, historically and personally, a crime committed by those who now rule Germany.

It is also the source of the terrible danger which threatens Germany like a colossal nightmare, imperilling both its existence as a State and its future as a nation.

For Hitler's decision to enter the road that leads to war, his reversion to the aims and methods of Prussian reactionary capitalism and imperialism, have conjured up a new worldwide coalition against Germany — a coalition whose deadly encirclement has once already led to a complete collapse of our country.

The almost insuperable severance of the German people from the world, the systematic leading of the populace astray by a fiendishly vertiginous propaganda, has hidden the real nature of the present situation. That situation is, in plain words, the following:

Should war ensue, no matter why or on what fronts, Germany will be faced by a worldwide coalition, led by England, France, Russia, and the Little Entente, while America, Poland, the Balkan Entente, and the Baltic Entente will constitute a reserve that will never decide for Germany, but in case of need will fight against her.

Of the reputed allies of Germany (Japan, Italy, Hungary, and Austria), it is possible that Japan will fulfil her pledges, will, that is to say, seize the chance, during the European complications, of strengthening her own position in the Far East; while the other powers named, with Italy at their head, will (in their own interest and from a sense of responsibility) remain neutral, especially during the decisive first weeks of the war.

Thus the result of the fateful and blind foreign policy of the Hitler System has been to establish a situation which, even though the German army should fight heroically and the German people prove ready for any sacrifices (provisos which, in existing circumstances, can by no means be relied upon), must inevitably result in the defeat of Germany.

Now what can this inevitable defeat of Germany mean other than the end of its political and economic independence, the end of its existence as a State. In a word, what can it mean other than the partition of Germany?

After losing a second World War, after a second Treaty of Versailles, there would only remain a powerless and disintegrated Germany, consisting of three or four dependent monarchies wholly subject to the dictatorial control of the victors.

In view of this situation, whose gravity makes us, the champions of the German Revolution, feel profoundly responsible, we have but one task:

To make an end of the Hitler System before it has destroyed Germany.

Every patriotic German, every German socialist above all, must recognize that Germany's life and future can only be safeguarded by making an end of the Hitler System before Germany is defeated.

Today to many of our fellow-countrymen these words, these perspectives, appear to be the outcome of needless panic; and perhaps the result of a phobia against the system, inspired by the morbid hate that fills refugees.

But tomorrow, when this forecast has been shockingly fulfilled, every German who loves his country and its people, every German nationalist and every German socialist, will be aware that the warnings of the Black Front have been and are justifiable, and all will echo our war-cry:

Down with the Hitler System before Germany is defeated.

Every officer of the Reich, every manual worker, every intellectual, and every peasant will then have to choose between Hitler and Germany, and we know that they will choose Germany.

Only in that case will the overthrow of the system be achieved without causing the defeat of Germany; and to the foreign governments and their peoples we urgently proclaim: 'A new Versailles could mean nothing but a fresh disaster for us and for you, since never will Germany renounce her unity and her freedom.'

But the guarantees that Europe will demand from Germany will be: in the negative sense, the overthrow of the Hitler System; and in the positive sense, the upbuilding of German socialism and the establishment of a European Federation.

The Black Front adjures the German people and the peoples of Europe to cling, before the war, during the war, and after the war, to these three aims:

National Freedom,
Social Justice,
European Collaboration.

# APPENDIXES

## NO GERMAN BLOOD FOR SPAIN

(Appeal of the Black Front to the German People)

Fellow-countrymen:

The rumours which for weeks have been spreading through Germany have of late been abundantly confirmed.

The Hitler System is selling more and more German soldiers, as mercenaries, to the Spanish generals.

Thousands upon thousands of young fellows, the best blood of Germany, are being shipped abroad, where they are fighting and dying, not to promote the national interests and the historical greatness of Germany, but on behalf of the reactionary party in a foreign civil war.

We accuse the Hitler System of this misuse of State authority, this squandering of irreplaceable national values. We accuse the Hitler System of deliberately injuring the German people, under the influence of partisan blindness and in the idiotic pursuit of prestige.

We ourselves do not take a side in the Spanish civil war. Just as we should repudiate any attempt by foreign powers to interfere in the home affairs of Germany, and would strenuously resist any invasion of our country by foreign mercenaries, so do we repudiate any German intervention in the home affairs of Spain, and most emphatically protest against the recruiting and use of German mercenaries on behalf of non-German interests.

This attitude, which must be a matter of principle for every sincere German nationalist, is reinforced by the fact that the German soldiers now being exported to Spain by the Hitler System are to be used there in favour of an economic and political reaction of the kind we ourselves have had to contend with for decades here in Germany, and to fight which is one of the main objects of genuine national socialism.

In its foreign policy of alliance with the Spanish reaction, the Hitler System is but reiterating its home policy of alliance with

233

the German reaction — a policy that led to the German Massacre of St. Bartholomew on June 30, 1934, and to the betrayal of German socialism.

National and socialist considerations make the fight against the sending of German troops to Spain one of the most important duties of every genuine National Socialist.

The Black Front therefore calls upon all true Germans, and especially upon all who belong to the Reichswehr, the S.S. [Storm-Guards], and the S.A. [Storm-Troops] to resist in every possible way this anti-national and anti-socialist policy of the Hitler System, under the slogans:

No German Blood for Spain,
Hail Germany.

On behalf of the German Black Front,
Otto Strasser

A CALL TO ARMS

(Watchword for the New Year, by Otto Strasser)

For two years the policy of the Hitler System has profited by the torpidity that seized poor old Europe after the consternating experiences of 1933. The system deliberately availed itself of the dread inspired by the prospect of a German Revolution, of the National Socialist renovation and renaissance of the German people, to stupefy capitalist Europe and scare it into inert neutrality. But this torpidity necessarily passed off, the spell was necessarily broken, when the alleged German Revolution disclosed itself to be no more than a desperate attempt on the part of the dominant classes to ensnare, slow down, strangle the revolution. The plainer it became to the governments of the victors of 1919 that the Hitler-Schacht-Goering-System lacked the inspiration of the revolutionary idea, that the wind of the revolutionary storm had blown over, that there was no genuinely creative revolutionary conception to animate the Continent, the more resolutely did they prepare for defence. When, after June 30, 1934, it became increasingly obvious to them that Hitler was playing the same cards as those which other statesmen had played before and were now playing beside him; that armaments, alliances, devices and momentary feints, opportunist combinations and veiled intrigues, were merely the pawns of his statecraft; but that he was nowise moved by a great idea able to revolutionize the old world, to procreate a new order in political and other human affairs, characterized by new laws and competent to produce new forms — the masters of old Europe, recognizing in Hitler a sprig of their own world degenerate, perhaps, and declassed, but still endeavouring to maintain the dominance of the bourgeoisie), saw that he was merely fighting them with familiar weapons on the familiar battlefield, and they prepared more vigorously than ever to resist.

Against the alliances of the Hitler System its adversaries first established the Franco-Russian Alliance which had nothing in common with bolshevism and communism, with Marxism and the revolution, but was merely a revival of the league, formed in 1894 and broken in 1917, between the two powers lying to the West and to the East against the hegemony of Central Europe.

The systematic consolidation of the Little Entente and the greater attention now paid by France to possible allies on the margin of Central Europe, with the resumption of cordial relations between France and Poland, were further stages of the defence against Hitler's policy of armament and treaty revision. But much the most dangerous measure was the systematic rearmament of Great Britain and the whole British Empire. During the years 1933-1936, nothing but the military weakness of England made it possible for Italian and German imperialism to achieve notable advances, and created situations in which England showed herself inert, or masked inertness by a badly simulated inattention towards the demand for treaty revision and the pugnacity of the other side. By now, in the beginning of 1937, England is getting ready to utter decisive words in international policy.

In order to set off the increasing activity of Western Europe, in 1936 Hitler and Mussolini began a counterstroke in Spain. The enterprise initiated by Generals Sanjurjo and Franco in July of that year (an enterprise they would never have ventured at that time unless they had come to an understanding with Berlin and Rome) was designed as a preventive occupation of what was ideologically, politically, and from the military stand-point the weakest point of Western Europe and of a future Franco-British coalition; it was a stab in the back for France, a preparation for a naval campaign against Britain. Actually for the time being the affair seemed to bode well for the interven-tionists. England was hampered by a dislike (based upon private capitalist interests) for the prospect of socialization of the Spanish mines, disinclined for anything that might lead to the U.S.S.R. getting established in the Western Mediterranean, and, being still only in the earlier stages of rearmament, again pretended to be blind and deaf, and let the reins drop. France, under the rule of the comparatively unstable popular front, could venture nothing without British aid. Russia, at first, was as neutral as the western powers. The generals, armed by Italy and Germany, were able to drive back the badly equipped and imperfectly trained militia of the Spanish government. A triumph of the Berlinese and of the Italian revisionary policy seemed assured. After three months, however, at long last, Russia began to intervene. Whether Moscow is moved by idealist promptings, stirred up by the internal pressure of the still unsettled struggle between Stalinism and Trotskyism, and wants to prevent the Spanish generals from gaining a complete victory, or is perhaps alarmed by the prospect of a political and military display on the Western European anti-Hitler front, it may be hard to decide. Anyhow the U.S.S.R. has intervened sufficiently in Spain to keep the fires of the civil war still burning briskly in mid-winter, so that a powerful reaction against the rebels remains possible. The military critics speak of what is going on in Spain as a 'Trial War', in which the soldiers of the great powers are fighting one another, and testing their up-to-date weapons. This remarkable civil war, fought on Spanish soil between Europeans of diverse nationalities under the command of Russian, German, and Italian officers, and using Russian, German, and Italian weapons, may develop into a general European war at any moment this year.

Hitler, who since 1934 has been captive of his own delusion, continues to believe that he has saved Europe from bolshevism, and that the nations of Europe are waiting for him to lead them upon an anti-Russian crusade, fancies that he could not find a more suitable occasion for war than this Spanish adventure. In his lunacy he overlooks the fact that between, on the one hand, the anti-bolshevik moods of the petty bourgeoisie, which throughout Europe sympathizes with the Spanish rebels, and, on the other, the motives which might induce the French, the British, and not least the Italian governments to allow themselves to be led into a decisive conflict, there lies all which he — the 'cork' of the revolution, the barometer of the German petty bourgeoisie, the idol of the masses, driven not driving, sentimentalist and somnambulist, no more than a pseudo-leader — is fundamentally incapable of understanding. The German generals understand well enough, and for weeks at Berchtesgaden have been fighting desperately against the Spanish adventure.

Whereas Mussolini continues to keep paths of withdrawal open, and should matters grow threatening would probably try to detach the fate of Italy from the fate of Germany, Hitler, mimicking the most preposterous fidelity, continues before all the world, through the mouth of Ward Price, to give General Franco pledges to the effect that Franco's cause is his own, and that no defeat of the Burgos government will be allowed. He really believes himself to be fighting against bolshevism and the popular front, and that the possible fall of Blum might induce France to take the side of Franco. But the very opposite is true, is absolutely certain. If Blum were to be replaced by Mandel, Chautemps, Pétain, any statesman of the Centre or the Right, France's attitude would only be stiffened, and it would become easier for Russia to invoke the aid of the Franco-Russian Alliance.

This winter Hitler's difficulties at home will be intensified to a pitch beyond anything that has been witnessed during the last few years, for they can only be paralleled by those of Germany, during the last war, between 1916 and 1918. For whereas in 1935 and 1936, after a difficult winter it was possible without serious risk to open the safety-valve of foreign policy, in March 1937 this safety-valve will probably have to take the form of war.

That will not merely be a matter of Hitler's political choice, for military considerations will likewise be operative. So bad is the prognosis for Germany that at the last moment a preventive war will very probably be begun, simply because it will be impossible to compete any longer with the heaping-up of armaments which has been going on in France, Russia, and England. For reasons that have frequently been stated here, Germany cannot now cope with it if Stalin should increase his standing army by another third of a million, if he transfers a hundred thousand more workers to the munition factories, if he places a yet larger quantity of raw materials at the disposal of the Red Army. Germany will not be able to compete should France devote her considerable gold reserve to further technical improvements in the army or to the construction of the Maginot line. Germany will have to take a back seat if England conjures up out of the ground a thousand more airplanes, gigantic battleships, whole fleets of destroyers and swift cruisers, huge squadrons of tanks. More and more risky becomes Goering's blitzkrieg in view of the titanic camps that surround Germany with inexhaustible arsenals, etc. The generals, who have recently discountenanced a military adventure, will soon have to decide whether to down Hitler, or to join Hitler in a leap into the dark, to venture the unknown depths of a preventive war.

But to down Hitler means to open the doors for the second revolution. The generals will not do this so long as Blomberg is supreme. Germany's fate today rests with Blomberg, with the life-or-death powers which, under Hitler's patronage, have been entrusted to the three dictators, Goering, Schacht, and Blomberg. The enormous powers which Hitler has granted to his vassal Blomberg is the leaden weight that paralyses the once influential Reichswehr. No longer can the Reichswehr decide against Hitler and for Germany; or, rather, it could only do so after Blomberg's fall. More and more improbable is it that an evolutionary possibility will be found, and decision by war looms as a bitter necessity.

In this war the new home political fronts will soon appear. The overwhelming odds that will face Germany in the struggle, the inevitable desertion of her expected allies, 'betrayal' by those friends upon whom Hitler and the people (deceived by Goebbels) count, the disastrous defeats that will certainly await the German army after its effective opening manœuvres, become plainer than they were in 1914 after the catastrophe on the Marne — plainer and more fulminant, for Germany no longer has ample reserves of men and stores of munitions for years of campaigning. This discloses the true situation of the German people, and demands a clear decision from the nation. In view of the millions of soldiers who will march against Germany from east and west and south, overshadowed by the bombing squadrons that will scatter death and destruction upon our towns and factories, stifled and strangled by a blockade that will cut us off from three-fourths of the world and deprive us of the raw materials most indispensable to war, the German people will have to choose between perishing, on the one hand, or, on the other, overthrowing the present system, and, under the sign of socialist renaissance, seeking enrolment in the community of western nations.

For this reason Hitler's mobilization must also be the signal for our own. For this reason we call the people to arms when Hitler calls them. We call them against Hitler, against the murderous Angel of Death to whom Hitler sacrifices Germany's young men, against pestilence and fire to which he will deliver Germany's towns and fields. We summon the people on behalf of Germany, on behalf of socialism, and in order to save Europe. During these years that are pregnant with fate we shall have no illusions, and we shall take the inevitable course of declaring war against Hitler when Hitler declares war; and to our comrades who in a few months will have to take up arms, we now have but two words to say:

'Get ready.'

# HUTTENBRIEF

## MANIFESTO OF THE BLACK FRONT TO THE GERMAN PEOPLE

[Ulrich von Hutten (1488-1533) was inspired throughout his short adult career by the aim of promoting a political and religious renaissance of Germany. His chief weapon was the pen, his chief medium consisted of letters, and he was probably one of the main authors of the famous *Epistolae obscurorum virorum*. His letters have become proverbial, and it was natural that the champions of the German Revolution in the twentieth century should claim to be speaking in the name of the man who laboured on behalf of a German — a European — Revolution four hundred years ago.]

### GREGOR STRASSER, THE HARBINGER OF GERMAN SOCIALISM

ON June 30, 1934, was murdered by Goering's orders (though Adolf Hitler, in the notorious Reichstag speech of July 13, 1934, frankly proclaimed his own responsibility) the man who, in conjunction with Moeller van den Bruck, may be regarded as chief herald and pioneer of German socialism — Gregor Strasser.

Through him alone it was that millions of Germans of both sexes made acquaintance with the new idea of national socialism. Hundreds of thousands of the members of the National Socialist Party knew him personally, the tall and vigorous man with a striking head, lucid eyes, and a powerful voice, who indefatigably preached the gospel of national socialism all over the country.

Tens of thousands had watched from close at hand his unceasing efforts on behalf of the party whose organization in North Germany was exclusively, and elsewhere in the Reich mainly, his work, which was done with that rare mingling of personal cordiality and unstinted zeal for toil that enabled him to move persons and master things. Thousands valued him as a friend, a helper in time of trouble, a leader into a new intellectual and spiritual world.

Not that he was ever a 'leader' in that superficial, arrogant, Byzantine style which later became typical of the party, when its soul had vanished and form had become all-important, demanding worship from idolaters. No, he was a leader of the spirit, a leader of the heart, a leader of endeavour.

It is not only because Gregor Strasser had so outstanding a personality that we wish to put a portrait of him before the nation to keep his memory fresh and vivid, but even more because his clear-sighted pursuit of an aim should never be forgotten, because his firmness of will should be a perennial warning, a promise, an example, and a consolation.

For in spite of, nay because of, Hitler's monstrous treason to the German people, it is needful, instructive, and comforting to keep our eyes fixed upon the lofty aim that was once put forward as that of the National Socialist Party, that National Socialist Party which in practice the Hitler System has so shamelessly betrayed, so basely desecrated.

German comrades and fellow-countrymen, sometime National Socialists and now party members, examine the books and writings, the speeches and pamphlets of Gregor Strasser, immerse yourselves in their words and their sense, read the 'inalterable' program of twenty-five points, and then turn back to consider what the Hitler System has actually been doing. In that way you will be enabled to grasp all the desolation of the German present.

You will perceive the most abominable fraud ever perpetrated upon believers, and you will understand why the henchmen of this system had the teacher and herald of German socialism put to death.

Like an inkling of the doom that awaited him sound the words which Gregor Strasser used as dedication for his master-work, *Kampf um Deutschland* [Fight for Germany]:

> *At one with them in will,*
> *I consecrate this book*
> *to those who have died*
> *for the movement*

In very truth it was for this German socialism that the fighters in the troubles of the post-war period went to their tombs. They died for the coming Germany of national freedom and social justice.

They did not die to promote the economic dictatorship of Schacht, Krupp, and Kirdorff; to establish the control of peoples' minds by Goebbels, Himmler, and Goering; to have our souls enslaved by Streicher, Rosenberg, and Kerrl.

That is why we pledge ourselves to these dead; why we pledge ourselves to Gregor Strasser who, having been the harbinger of German Socialism, became its martyr; why we solemnly swear.

The Hitler System shall perish.
German Socialism shall survive.

Otto Strasser

## FIGHT FOR GERMANY

### by Gregor Strasser

*Editorial Introduction: Gregor Strasser's own words will demonstrate, better than we could hope to do by anything that we could write, his creative importance to German socialism.*

*We therefore extract from his* Kampf um Deutschland, *published in 1932 by the official Eher-Verlag, the following passages which incor-*

*porate his guiding principles, and adjure all genuine National Socialists to compare with the aims of National Socialism, as thus expounded, the actual deeds of the Hitler System.*

We National Socialists are socialists, genuine, national, German socialists. We repudiate any attempt to tone down this idea by using the word 'social reformer' instead of the word 'socialist'. This change of wording represents nothing but a hypocritical attempt to hide the most glaring defects of the capitalist economic system. Or at best it can be regarded as the endeavour of compassionate and honourable persons to cure, by covering them up with plaster, the festering sores on the body of our economic life and of our people. We are 'socialists', and not mere 'social reformers', and we do not hesitate to say it, although the Marxians have so painfully distorted the meaning of the former term.

What do we mean when we call ourselves National Socialists; and why are we National Socialists?

We start from the idea that a nation is made up of persons who have a community of fates. Now to have a community of fates signifies that there must be a community of needs, and if there is a community of needs there must be a community of bread.

The nationalist movement joins us in recognizing that there is a community of fates and a community of needs, but calls a halt when we say this necessarily means a community of bread. A community of bread signifies that the land, its treasures, and its powers, are the property of the entire people, of the entire nation. That is the significance of the misleading Marxian expression 'ownership of the means of production'. For not any one class, not even the working class, owns the means of production. The owner is the nation as a whole. (Pp. 72-73.)

That denotes revolution — an economic revolution? Certainly it does. We want this economic revolution, just as Baron vom Stein once wanted an economic revolution, and made it, to secure the national freedom of the German people. For what else but an immense economic revolution was the widespread liberation of the serfs — a revolution which the feudal magnates of those days would certainly have described (if the word had already existed) as 'bolshevik', and which they did describe as 'a danger to the State' — even as our National Socialist demand is now described in capitalist circles. Only thanks to the economic revolution of the liberation of the serfs, only through the incorporation of the newly established system of estates into the calcified organism of the State, were freed the mighty forces that were requisite; only thanks to this did the Prussia of 1806 become the Prussia of 1812 and the Germany of 1870. Moreover it is our profound conviction that in no other way than by the liberation of the fourth estate, by the incorporation of the German working class into the organism of the German nation, can the Germany of 1918 be transformed into the free Germany of a near and the Great Germany of a more distant future. (Pp. 74-75.)

We National Socialists perceive that there is a fateful and causal tie between the national liberty of our people and the economic emancipation of the German workers. We have recognized that the capitalist economic system with its exploitation of those who are economically weak, with its robbery of the workers' labour-power, with its unethical way of appraising human beings by the number of things and the amount of money they possess, instead of by their internal value and their achievements, must be replaced by a new and just economic system, in a word by German socialism. The basic idea of socialism which, though Hebraically falsified, materialistically degraded, and demagogically caricatured, nevertheless lives on in the minds of millions upon millions of social-democratic and communist workers, that ancient Teutonic notion of joint ownership by the whole tribe, by the whole nation, of the entire means of production, of the land, which the individual who tills it holds only in 'entail', as a usufructuary entrusted with his farm by the community — such is the rock-bottom upon which our wish to refashion economic life is grounded. This conviction, which is so deeply rooted in individual hearts that even a capitalistically inclined person really accepts it in his inmost self, supplies the motive force to our National Socialist idea of economics, society, and the State. (Pp. 101-102.)

We have to learn that work is more than possession, that achievement is more than dividends. The most deplorable legacy of the capitalist economic system is that it has taught us to judge all things by the standards of money, ownership, possession. The decay of a people is a necessary outcome of applying such a standard of value, for selection by ownership is the mortal foe of the race, of blood, and of life. We have no shadow of doubt that under National Socialism this privilege of ownership will be annulled, and that the liberation of the German worker will go so far as to include a share in profit, a share in ownership, and a share in management. But we shall not have escaped from the old standard of value if we leave matters there, without insisting upon that revolution in the mind which impels us to our assault upon the spirit of the present system. We deliberately change from valuation by ownership to valuation by achievement, this latter being our sole standard. For us achievement is the main point, not dividend, just as we consider responsibility, rather than wealth or display, to be the climax of human endeavour. Here we have a new outlook, a new religion for economic life. Thanks to this the worship of the golden calf will come to an end; the differences between human beings and the differences between their rights will be differences between their achievements, differences in the degrees of their responsibility, differences that come from God and are therefore sacred. (Pp. 132-133.)

# APPENDIXES

In the people's movement there is much talk about the crystallizing of a new leadership, and this touches upon what I have just been saying. But the methods that have been suggested for coming to a decision as to the best leaders, such as examination of the blood, and what not, seem to my practical mind rather dubious, as to their possibility, their use, and their effect. There is another plan, an Old-German, a Prussian plan, of which my friend Pfeffer has reminded me, and which seems to me admirable. I mean, choice based upon the army.

As a preliminary to the use of this method, service in the army must be voluntary — a privilege and not a duty. The practical plan would be to provide by law that every German citizen must do State service for a year. What I propose is that during this year he should not be set to roadmaking or some other sort of mass-labour, but should be taught a handicraft, so that there should be no grown-up Germans who had not received at least one year's training in some craft or other. But the choice of the best would be left to apply to those who, after the year's 'civil service', chose to volunteer for the army. Army service would last several years, and, apart from this, it would only attract self-sacrificing persons, inasmuch as it would involve the chance of being exposed to the perils of war, and would therefore call for the heroic virtues. But, I repeat, to adopt service in the army would be left voluntary and unconstrained. Who can doubt that those Germans who volunteered for military service, which would take them away from private life for at least twice as long as the civil service did, would give no practical advantages for vocational life, but which besides being much harder work, would entail upon the volunteer all the risks of war — who can doubt, I say, that such Germans as these volunteers would be the best Germans, racially the best, whose achievements on behalf of the State now and in the future would enormously transcend those of the average man? (Pp. 134-135.)

The souls of human beings are overshadowed by a terrible hopelessness. Fixed values have been crumbling away. People don't know what to cling to, and vainly seek a centre of gravity, which they have lost in morals, and cannot find in religion. 'Relativity' has become the shibboleth of modern culture, the relativity of all things, of all knowledge, of all feelings. Vainly does the sufferer try to escape the dull anxiety of an uneasy conscience, try to mask and to excuse his instability with the aid of psychoanalysis. The core has been gnawed at until very little of it remains.

This is the sorest wound, perhaps incurable. For it is a profound truth that moral health is indispensable to the social and political stability of a people. Don't let the reader misunderstand me when I use the word 'moral'. Morality cannot be established upon any other foundation than the soul, cannot be sustained by any reputedly inalterable commandments, even though to begin with these commandments were fortified with a sort of 'extract of the soul'. We are not concerned here with the dogmatic morality proclaimed by an estate or by a religion, but with the harmony that prevails (or should prevail) between eternal nature and that which is divine in man. The form, therefore, is temporal, like man himself; but the content, the soul, is eternal. (Pp. 137-138.)

You German workers number fifteen millions. With your dependents you comprise 85% of the German people. Why, then, should you tolerate having to suffer all through life, every hour of every day, from the most horrible anxiety about the morrow, the dread whether next pay-day, or on the first of next month, you will still have enough money to provide you and yours with food, clothing, and shelter.

Why should you put up, year after year, with the most poignant anxiety about old age, having continually to ask yourselves: 'What on earth shall I do when I am no longer able to work?' Why do you endure having all the joys of life — the founding of a family, the upbringing of happy, healthy children — poisoned by the tyranny of a system that mercilessly exploits you, and treats you as slaves? Why should you stand having life's lesser pleasures — reverie in a wood, choosing a toy for the baby — spoiled, once more, by the tyranny of money?

Why do you put up with this servile existence which robs you of human dignity; cuts you off from the happiness of life; and converts that life of yours, which according to the eternal laws of nature and the eternal rights of man ought to be a psalm of praise to the Almighty, into a scream of hatred for the devil, a wail of sorrow and despair, of poverty and disgust and death.

Why do you bear it, brothers and sisters?

Because they lie to you and cheat you, cloud your vision so that you fail to see the enemy who afflicts you with all your woes. Because your hearts and brains are so drugged that you quarrel with one another instead of joining forces against that enemy: the unemployed has a grudge against the employed; the manual operative against the brainworker; the townsman against the agricultural labourer; the countryman against the official; and so on and so forth. Because you let them incite you against one another: the communists against the social democrats, both of them against the 'bourgeois'; the soldier against the civilian; the Red Front men against those who wear the Swastika. But aren't you comrades, comrades in misfortune, 'brothers of the chain'? Is not the same whip cracked in the ears of you all, are not you scourged by the same dread of poverty? Are not your lives unhappy enough already, without these quarrels? Are not you universally defrauded of the Rights of Man? (Pp. 146-148.)

We should not be socialists if we were unwilling to fight against the class-rule of the capitalist system, which permits a class of citizens whose only title is one of ownership to decide the lives and the deaths of the great majority of their fellow-citizens. But we should not be nationalists if we were not no less passionately determined to repudiate the hateful attempt to turn matters upside-down at the will of the brutalized masses of those who have hitherto been under the harrow, and are now unable to recognize the impossibility of detaching the fortunes of one class (be it a small minority or a large majority) from the fortunes of the nation. For here is our great discovery, that true socialism is identical with true nationalism, both being equally hostile to the class rule of a privileged bourgeoisie and the class rule of the proletariat.

What do we want, then? Neither the 'bourgeois' nor yet the 'proletarians' — neither the bourgeois State nor yet the proletarian State. We want a new kind of man, we want the State of these new human beings who evoke in its pristine purity from the bourgeoisie the idea of nationalism which issues from the depths of the blood; and evoke from the proletariat the idea of socialism, redoubled in strength by the injustice the proletarians have suffered. We want all the champions from both camps who have discovered within themselves the synthesis that bridges the formidable abyss which now yawns between the two camps; that synthesis of the new idea which teaches us to be socialists because we are nationalists, and to be nationalists because we are socialists

Like a fate it lowers over German history, which is an outflow of the struggle of the German soul on behalf of itself and to find itself — this surge of mutual hatreds, this murderous struggle of brother against brother for the sake of an idea which remains unknown to most of the combatants until, after the most fearful birthpangs, it is born in the synthesis which was something new and nevertheless embodied what was best in both the contesting parties: in the Guelph-Ghibelline synthesis of the Holy Roman Empire of the German Nation; in the Papist-Lutheran synthesis of the lesser German empire which secured its definitive configuration through Bismarck; in the Bourgeois-Proletarian synthesis of the coming Third Reich of national liberty and social justice. (Pp. 165-166.)

# GREGOR STRASSER'S LEGACY

MUNICH, FEBRUARY 6, 1933

MANY thanks for your letter of the 3rd inst. I am always glad to hear from you, and to know that the group holds firmly together. It is my hope and my earnest wish that the 'Strasser Case' will not lead to any change in this respect. The newspapers will have kept you acquainted with the political situation in Germany. In the end I and my political views have won, for I felt that, whatever happened, the N.S.D.A.P. [National Socialist Party] ought to be incorporated in the State. This has happened, in part because of my direct efforts, and to some extent because the party was afraid of me. To all appearance I may seem to have been left out in the cold, but inwardly I don't feel this, for the renunciation of all economic ministries (which are in the hands of the arch-reactionary Hugenberg), and of the Prussian instruments of power (which are in the hands of the much-reviled Papen), may indeed promote the national aims of the National Socialists, but will not further what we call German socialism — and that, I am firmly convinced, is what the future will demand. My time will come when in Germany the power of the great financiers and the great landowners has to be broken; no matter whether it is done with the aid of the N.S.D.A.P. by currency methods, or by establishing the political front in a new form and with new energies.

What perturbs me rather, from time to time at least, is the fact that, by various intrigues, some of the subordinate leaders, ambitious or otherwise shady persons, have been dragging my name and honour in the mire by unprecedented misstatements and infamies. But I shall keep my end up all right, and after a while even exasperated people will come to understand the reasons that have moved me and the general soundness of my conduct. The conversation that was arranged for has been postponed by Hitler. Since meanwhile he has become Chan-

Lightning Source UK Ltd.
Milton Keynes UK
UKHW02f1912170518
322795UK00005B/302/P